# THE ITT CORE CONTENT FRAMEWORK

Sara Miller McCune founded Sage Publishing in 1965 to support the dissemination of usable knowledge and educate a global community. Sage publishes more than 1000 journals and over 800 new books each year, spanning a wide range of subject areas. Our growing selection of library products includes archives, data, case studies and video. Sage remains majority owned by our founder and after her lifetime will become owned by a charitable trust that secures the company's continued independence.

Los Angeles | London | New Delhi | Singapore | Washington DC | Melbourne

JONATHAN GLAZZARD AND SAMUEL STONES

# THE ITT CORE CONTENT FRAMEWORK

## WHAT TRAINEE PRIMARY SCHOOL TEACHERS NEED TO KNOW

2ND EDITION

Learning Matters

Learning Matters
A Sage Publishing Company
1 Oliver's Yard
55 City Road
London EC1Y 1SP

Sage Publications Inc.
2455 Teller Road
Thousand Oaks, California 91320

Sage Publications India Pvt Ltd
B 1/I 1 Mohan Cooperative Industrial Area
Mathura Road
New Delhi 110 044

Sage Publications Asia-Pacific Pte Ltd
3 Church Street
#10-04 Samsung Hub
Singapore 049483

Editor: Amy Thornton
Senior project editor: Chris Marke
Project management: TNQ Tech Pvt. Ltd.
Cover design: Wendy Scott
Typeset by: TNQ Tech Pvt. Ltd.
Printed in the UK


First published in 2020

Second edition published in 2024



**Library of Congress Control Number: 2023947905**

**British Library Cataloguing in Publication Data**

A catalogue record for this book is available from the British Library

ISBN 978-1-5296-7192-6
ISBN 978-1-5296-7193-3 (pbk)

# CONTENTS

# ABOUT THE AUTHORS

**Jonathan Glazzard** holds the Rosalind Hollis Professorship in Education for Social Justice in the School of Education at the University of Hull. He has been a teacher educator for 18 years, working in five universities across Yorkshire, the Humber and the North West of England. He worked as a teacher in schools for 10 years prior to his career in higher education. Jonathan's research focuses on illuminating the experiences of people on the margins of society. He is an experienced researcher. Recent projects include international perspectives on LGBTQ+ inclusion in education, the well-being of children and educators, the experiences of young, disabled people who are queer and educational and life transitions of LGBTQ+ students in higher education. He is committed to researching *with* rather than *on* individuals, groups and communities and his research adopts a strong participatory approach.

**Samuel Stones** is a doctoral student, Lecturer and researcher in the Carnegie School of Education at Leeds Beckett University. His research outputs are linked with the Centre for LGBTQ+ Inclusion in Education and the Carnegie Centre of Excellence for Mental Health in Schools. Samuel currently supervises dissertation students on a range of postgraduate courses, and he works with initial teacher training students in university and school contexts. Samuel is also an Assistant Headteacher at a school and sixth form college in North Yorkshire where he oversees curriculum and assessment.

# ABOUT THIS BOOK

This book addresses the *Initial Teacher Training Core Content Framework*. This framework outlines the essential knowledge and skills that trainee teachers need to develop during their initial teacher education course. The framework is aligned to the *Teachers' Standards*, but includes further detail about precisely what trainees need to know, understand and be able to do. This book is intended to be used by primary trainee teachers on primary 5–11 teacher training courses.

The book is structured in line with the framework and the *Teachers' Standards*. However, rather than interpreting the standards as distinct from each other, it is important that you understand their interrelatedness. Effective behaviour management (TS7) supports pupils to make good progress (TS2). Good progress (TS2) is also supported by demonstrating high expectations of learners (TS1), good subject knowledge (TS3), carefully structured lessons and pedagogical approaches (TS4), inclusive teaching (TS5), effective use of assessment (TS6) and effective deployment of teaching assistants (TS8). All the standards therefore support pupil progress.

As you move through your initial teacher training, you will gradually develop new knowledge and skills. Your knowledge and skills will be supported by tutors, school-based mentors, other teachers in school and the wider education community and personal research. It is important that you take responsibility for your own professional development. Teaching is a challenging yet deeply rewarding profession. You should be prepared to be reflective and take risks in your practice. At the same time, it is important not to be afraid to seek advice and ask for help when you need it.

At this stage in your development (and at all stages of your career), it is important to view yourself as both a teacher and a learner. Working in different schools, with different classes of children of varying ages will inevitably test you. There are rarely any right or wrong 'answers' in teaching, but certainly many shades of grey. What works with one pupil or one class may not work for another. Be willing to try different strategies, implement and evaluate them. You will experience a great deal of success, but you will also experience lessons, days and sometimes weeks when things seem to be going drastically wrong. Do not despair. In teaching, no two days (or two pupils) are the same. This is what makes teaching so exhilarating. However, when things go wrong, it is all too easy to take things personally and to blame yourself. In these situations, try to learn from what you have experienced.

Try not to dwell on things and use all your experiences (good and bad) to shape your development as a teacher. Effective teachers continually view themselves as learners. They consistently reflect on their practice and solve problems as they occur. When things get bad, talk to others – your peers, tutors and other teachers. We all experience days where the last place we want to be is in a school. On days like this, remember why you decided to become a teacher. It provides you with a direct opportunity to influence children's futures, to change values, attitudes and beliefs, and to make a real difference.

This book provides you with some key knowledge that you will find useful. However, one book cannot cover everything you need to do. This book attempts to introduce you to the key knowledge that you need, but you will want to research some aspects in greater depth. Each chapter includes links to research and practical classroom examples that will help you to contextualise the theories and literature. Your understanding of the core content needs to be underpinned with rich and sustained periods of time in school, which will enable you to apply your knowledge of the framework within your practice.

# TRAINING TO TEACH

## THINGS TO REMEMBER

- [ ] Take responsibility for your own professional development.
- [ ] Be prepared to be reflective and take risks in your practice.
- [ ] Do not be afraid to seek advice and ask for help when you need it.
- [ ] Remember, you are both a teacher and a learner.
- [ ] There are rarely any right or wrong 'answers' in teaching, but certainly many shades of grey.
- [ ] What works with one pupil or one class may not work for another.
- [ ] Be willing to try different strategies, to implement them and evaluate them.
- [ ] You will experience a great deal of success, but you will also experience lessons, days and sometimes weeks when things seem to be going drastically wrong.
- [ ] Do not despair. In teaching no two days (or two pupils) are the same.
- [ ] Try not to take things personally and to blame yourself.
- [ ] Try not to dwell on things and use all your experiences (good and bad) to shape your development as a teacher.
- [ ] When things get bad, talk to others - your peers, tutors and other teachers.
- [ ] We all experience days where the last place we want to be is in a school. On days like this, remember why you decided to become a teacher.
- [ ] Teaching provides you with a direct opportunity to influence children's futures, to change values, attitudes and beliefs and to make a real difference.

# INTRODUCTION

## WHAT DOES THE *ITT CORE CONTENT FRAMEWORK* MEAN FOR TEACHER EDUCATORS AND TRAINEE TEACHERS?

### IN THIS CHAPTER

This chapter outlines the *ITT Core Content Framework*. It introduces you to the framework and provides you with some background information about its development. This chapter is mainly intended for ITT providers and their partnerships rather than for trainees, although it is likely that trainees will find the implications of the framework interesting in relation to their own professional practice.

## KEY RESEARCH

The *ITT Core Content Framework* (DfE/EEF, 2019) was developed from the *Carter Review of Initial Teacher Training (ITT)* (Carter, 2015), which made some key recommendations for ITT courses. Key recommendations from this review are identified below:

- To develop a framework of core ITT content.
- Subject knowledge and subject-specific pedagogy should be included in this framework.
- The framework should include a strong emphasis on evidence-based teaching.
- Theories of assessment should be included in this framework.
- Child and adolescent development should be included.
- The framework should include practical strategies to support trainees in managing pupils' behaviour.

- Special educational needs and disabilities should be included in the framework.
- Trainees require input on developing their professionalism, resilience and time management.

(Carter, 2015)

## KEY POLICY

The *ITT Core Content Framework* states:

> *The quality of teaching is the single most important in-school factor in improving outcomes for pupils – and it is particularly important for pupils from disadvantaged backgrounds. No one is born a great teacher. Great teachers continuously improve over time, benefitting from the mentoring of expert colleagues and a structured introduction to the core body of knowledge, skills and behaviours that define great teaching.*
>
> (DfE/EEF, 2019, p3)

The *ITT Core Content Framework* (DfE/EEF, 2019) sets out the minimum entitlement for trainee teachers. It draws on the best available evidence from research to identify the elements of quality-first teaching. The framework does not identify all the content that trainee teachers need, and neither is it a curriculum. This is because it is not sequenced, and it does not identify the components of knowledge that trainee teachers need to learn. Providers will need to make decisions about how to structure the content to provide trainees with a well-sequenced, coherent ITT curriculum. It is a framework that sets out the minimum essential knowledge and skills that trainee teachers need to become effective teachers. Together with the *Early Career Framework* (DfE, 2019a), it will provide a comprehensive package of support for teachers at the early stages of their careers.

The *ITT Core Content Framework* should not be used as an assessment framework to assess the performance of trainee teachers. Although it aligns with the *Teachers' Standards* (DfE, 2011), it emphasises specific essential knowledge for trainees. Building on the recommendations of the *Carter Review of Initial Teacher Training* (Carter, 2015), there is a strong emphasis on developing trainees' knowledge of behaviour management and special educational needs. In addition, there is a strong emphasis on developing trainees' subject knowledge. The framework emphasises the importance of subject- and age-specific training because strong subject knowledge is associated with good outcomes for pupils (Coe et al., 2014).

In addition, the framework emphasises the importance of providing quality-first teaching for all pupils. It explicitly states that:

> The quality of teaching is the single most important in-school factor in improving outcomes for pupils – and it is particularly important for pupils from disadvantaged backgrounds. No one is born a great teacher. Great teachers continuously improve over time, benefitting from the mentoring of expert colleagues and a structured introduction to the core body of knowledge, skills and behaviours that define great teaching.
>
> (DfE/EEF, 2019, p.3)

> *The ITT Core Content Framework is deliberately designed to emphasise the importance of high-quality teaching, which is particularly important for disadvantaged pupils and those with additional needs. For this reason, the ITT Core Content Framework deliberately does not detail approaches specific to particular additional needs – to reflect the importance of quality first teaching.*
>
> (DfE/EEF, 2019, p6)

There is a strong emphasis on providing all pupils with high-quality teaching. The framework states that this is the best way of raising outcomes for disadvantaged pupils and those with special educational needs and/or disabilities. The framework therefore does not emphasise the use of differentiated approaches because these can serve to widen ability gaps between groups of pupils. There is also an emphasis on developing trainees' understanding of how to support pupils with specific mental health needs. For primary schools, the framework specifically emphasises the importance of developing trainees' knowledge and understanding of systematic synthetic phonics to support pupils' early reading development. In addition, there is an emphasis on developing trainees' subject knowledge in mathematics.

In line with the *Education Inspection Framework* (Ofsted, 2023), the framework includes an emphasis on supporting trainees to manage their workloads and their own well-being.

## WHAT DOES THE *ITT CORE CONTENT FRAMEWORK* MEAN FOR TRAINEES?

Although the *ITT Core Content Framework* should not be used as an assessment framework to evaluate your capability as a teacher, nonetheless it breaks down the *Teachers' Standards* into more specific content that you need to know and understand. You can use it as a developmental framework to identify things that you already know and understand, and aspects that you need to develop. Once you have identified these aspects, you can focus discussions with your mentors on how to address these aspects within your practice. You can also observe other teachers to see how they implement these aspects in their practice. If you use the *ITT Core Content Framework* in this way, it becomes a tool to support your development as a teacher.

## WHAT DOES THE *ITT CORE CONTENT FRAMEWORK* MEAN FOR COURSE MANAGERS AND TUTORS?

Trainers should ensure that all the aspects of the *ITT Core Content Framework* are embedded within either central training or school-based training and as well as being delivered separately, the content in the Core Content Framework (CCF) should be purposefully integrated into subjects. Trainers should work collaboratively with their partnership schools to map how aspects of the framework which are delivered centrally are supported or further developed through school-based training. Some aspects might be delivered solely centrally, others might be delivered solely by schools, and some aspects can be delivered both in school and centrally.

## WHAT DOES THE *ITT CORE CONTENT FRAMEWORK* MEAN FOR MENTORS?

The *ITT Core Content Framework* includes the minimum knowledge that trainee teachers need to know and understand. Providers should work collaboratively with schools across their partnerships to jointly plan a coherent curriculum for trainee teachers. Some aspects of the framework can be delivered by school-based mentors and other aspects can be delivered by centrally-based trainers who are not in schools – for example, lecturers.

School-based mentors play a critical role in supporting trainees to apply their theoretical understanding of the content to practical contexts. It is not enough for trainees to know the theories that underpin the key aspects of the framework. Trainee teachers ultimately need to be able to develop the skills to apply their learning in practical situations. This is why one complete strand of the CCF focuses on *'learn how to'*. School-based mentors can support trainees to develop practical teaching skills using processes such as coaching and mentoring.

### TAKE 5

- The *ITT Core Content Framework* identifies the content which is a minimum entitlement for trainees.
- Providers must not use it as an ITT curriculum.
- Providers must sequence the content logically to provide trainees with a coherent curriculum.
- There is a strong emphasis on behaviour management, subject knowledge and quality-first teaching for all pupils in the framework.
- The *ITT Core Content Framework*, in conjunction with the *Early Career Framework*, provides early career teachers with a coherent programme of professional development in the early stages of their careers.

## SUMMARY

This chapter has introduced the *ITT Core Content Framework* and the minimum entitlements it provides to all trainee teachers. The underpinning research has been outlined and the implications for mentors have been discussed. However, it is essential that ITT providers remember that the framework does not set out the full ITT curriculum for trainee teachers. Individual providers must still design a curriculum that is appropriate for the subject, phase and age range that trainees will be teaching. It is, therefore, crucially important that providers ensure that trainees have the foundational knowledge and skills that are required to access and understand the content within the framework. Furthermore, providers must identify and sequence components of knowledge that underpin the broader goals of the CCF. Providers must ensure that their curriculums provide trainees with the full entitlement outlined in the framework as well as designing curriculums that go beyond the minimum requirements.

# 1

# HIGH EXPECTATIONS

**IN THIS CHAPTER**

It is essential that teachers have high expectations of all pupils. Teachers' beliefs in relation to their pupils and what they can achieve can have a substantial impact on pupil learning. These beliefs are also likely to influence pedagogical approaches and the extent to which pupils are exposed to cognitively demanding experiences and advanced learning opportunities. To support your understanding, this chapter reviews existing research on pedagogy, and teaching and learning, and it offers some practical guidance in relation to professional practice. It also outlines the importance of demonstrating high standards of professional behaviour and your role in fostering pupils' well-being, motivation and behaviour.

## KEY RESEARCH

According to Coe et al. (2014), evidence of pedagogical approaches that produce a strong impact on children's progress

> *include elements such as effective questioning and the use of assessment by teachers. Specific practices, like reviewing previous learning, providing model responses for students, giving adequate time for practice to embed skills securely and progressively introducing new learning (scaffolding) are also elements of high-quality instruction.*
>
> (Coe et al., 2014, pp2–3)

These teaching strategies will impact most positively on your pupils. It is essential that you have high expectations of every child, irrespective of their social background or other circumstances. Children will rise to your expectations. If your expectations are too low, they will underachieve. It is important that you foster a sense of self-belief in children. There might be aspects of subject content that they struggle to master initially.

However, it is your role to help them to recognise that with continued effort and persistence, they will be able to master that content and achieve a high level.

Your lessons should include appropriate learning challenges so that pupils make good progress and do not become disengaged. It is important not to underestimate what children are capable of because often they will surprise you. Setting lower-level tasks for children with special educational needs can demonstrate to children that you have low expectations of their capabilities. If you increase your expectations, develop their self-belief and support them to achieve suitable learning challenges, then you will start to narrow discrepancies in achievement between different groups of pupils. Developing a belief that all children can achieve highly, irrespective of social background and other circumstances, should be fundamental to your values as a teacher.

## KEY POLICY

The *Teachers' Standards* state that teachers must:

- *establish a safe and stimulating environment for pupils, rooted in mutual respect.*
- *set goals that stretch and challenge pupils of all backgrounds, abilities and dispositions.*
- *demonstrate consistently the positive attitudes, values and behaviour which are expected of pupils.*

(DfE, 2011)

## 1.1 BEING A ROLE MODEL

Being a role model places a responsibility on you to consistently demonstrate the highest standards of professional behaviour. You should treat children with respect and kindness, even when they do not replicate this towards you. If children are rude, defiant or aggressive, this is rarely personal. There may be complex reasons that underpin their behaviour, and it is important that you respond to challenging behaviour in a calm, controlled and professional manner. Some children will be continually exposed to models of aggression at home, and it is critical that they are exposed to alternative responses from adults who are positive role models.

As a role model to children, you should also:

- be punctual at school and lessons.
- listen to children when they communicate with you.
- address negative behaviour firmly but calmly.

- demonstrate professional dress and use of language.
- maintain professional boundaries while being friendly.
- apologise when you get things wrong.
- believe that they can achieve and communicate this belief to them.
- believe that they can improve their behaviour and communicate this belief to them.
- maintain good attendance.
- ensure that lessons are planned, organised and ready to run when children enter the room.
- encourage children to take ownership of their learning environment.
- refrain from any form of substance use in front of children – for example, smoking cigarettes outside of school.

## 1.2 LEARNING TO BE A PROFESSIONAL

Some of the aspects of learning to be a professional have been outlined in the section above. Your experience of being a pupil in school is likely to be relatively recent. The moment you begin a course of initial teacher education you need to adopt a professional persona. You should recognise that you are learning to be a professional and you should understand what this process entails. You should be willing to listen to advice and act on feedback. This is essential to your success as a trainee teacher. You should also be willing to reflect frequently on your own strengths and weaknesses and be proactive in continually improving your teaching. No one will expect you to be perfect, but everyone will expect you to be willing to learn. You should be prepared to ask questions to further your own understanding, and you should be prepared to participate fully in training sessions and other forms of professional learning to fully benefit from your teacher education course.

You should review your social media profiles to ensure that they do not include content that might potentially bring your schools or teacher education provider into disrepute. In addition, you should adjust your behaviour outside of school in your personal life to ensure that this does not lead others to question your suitability as a teacher.

Make the most of your time in school. Take opportunities to observe a range of experienced teachers in the classroom. Ask questions, particularly if you need clarification. Research into the subject content that you are required to teach and establish links with other professionals on social media. This is a useful way of seeking support and sharing resources. Accept that you will never be the finished product. Learning to be a teacher is a lifelong process. It does not end when you complete your teacher education course. One of the joys of teaching is that you will be continually learning and continually improving your practice. Recognise that you can learn different things from different people and be open-minded. Accept that your previous academic success does not guarantee you success in the teaching profession. You will make mistakes, and you will have strengths and weaknesses, and your performance can change as you move between different school contexts and year groups.

## 1.3 HOW TEACHERS AFFECT PUPIL WELL-BEING, MOTIVATION AND BEHAVIOUR

Teachers play a crucial role in fostering good well-being, motivation and behaviour in their pupils. If your own well-being is poor, this can impact on the well-being of your pupils. As professionals, we recognise that life is not always easy. There may be circumstances in your personal or professional lives which impact on your well-being. Looking after yourself is important, not only for you but also for your pupils. Many children experience adverse circumstances at home. School should be a place where they can consistently enjoy learning, be happy, feel safe and experience a sense of belonging. If your own well-being is poor, it might be more appropriate to take some time out and get support rather than attempt to continue teaching when you are not well. Your teacher education provider has a responsibility to support your well-being.

Research suggests that there appears to be a causal relationship between teacher and pupil mental health (Harding et al., 2019). Positive teacher–pupil relationships support children and young people to be mentally healthy (Kidger et al., 2012; Plenty et al., 2014). These relationships help children to feel more connected to their school (Harding et al., 2019) and improve their well-being (Aldridge and McChesney, 2018) through fostering a sense of belonging. Research demonstrates that teachers with poor mental health may find it more difficult to develop and model positive relationships with their pupils (Jennings and Greenberg, 2009; Kidger et al., 2010).

School is also a place where pupils can be exposed to high expectations in relation to their behaviour. Some pupils will experience inconsistent boundaries from

# MAKE THE MOST OF YOUR TIME IN SCHOOL ...

- [ ] Take opportunities to observe a range of experienced teachers in the classroom.
- [ ] Ask questions.
- [ ] Research the subject content that you are required to teach.
- [ ] Establish links with other professionals on social media (this is a useful way of seeking support and for sharing resources).
- [ ] Accept that you will never be the finished product. Learning to be a teacher is a lifelong process. It does not end when you complete your teacher education course.
- [ ] Recognise that you can learn different things from different people and be open-minded.
- [ ] Accept that your previous academic success does not guarantee you success in the teaching profession.
- [ ] You will make mistakes and you will have strengths and weaknesses and your performance can change as you move between different school contexts and year groups.

parents, and they will need time to adjust their behaviour to the expectations of the school context. Supporting pupils to recognise their emotions and regulate them is one of your responsibilities as a teacher. Addressing the consequences of poor behaviour is rarely enough. Children's behaviour is often a response to an unmet need. You should therefore aim to understand what the child is trying to communicate through their behaviour rather than interpreting poor behaviour as a sign of weakness. Demonstrating empathy and patience will serve you well in teaching.

You will naturally seek to provide lessons that motivate and inspire your learners. Planning tasks that are stimulating and provide opportunities for learning through collaboration and investigation will help you to foster motivation. In addition, planning opportunities for pupils to engage with a broad curriculum will ensure that they can develop interests in a range of subjects.

## 1.4 SETTING GOALS THAT STRETCH AND CHALLENGE PUPILS

During your lessons, you are responsible for ensuring that all children are appropriately challenged so that they make good or better progress. In particular, you will need to ensure that children who are operating at lower stages of cognitive development are not given lower-level tasks that result in widening the ability gap between them and their peers. Where appropriate, you should consider how these children might be supported to achieve the same learning outcomes as their peers by providing them with additional adult support, and different resources or by breaking the task down further into smaller steps. It might not always be appropriate for children who are working at lower stages of development to work on the same learning objectives as their peers who are operating at higher stages of development, but setting a different task should not be the default 'fall-back' position.

You will need to consider how you will meet the needs of children who are operating at higher stages of cognitive development. You can challenge them further by setting them extension tasks or by asking them to apply the skill or concept that you have taught them. Sometimes, it will be appropriate to set these children a completely different task from their peers, provided they are secure with the prerequisite subject content. It is counterproductive to move children on too quickly, particularly if the prerequisite knowledge, skills and understanding required to complete the task are not secure. To ensure an appropriate level of challenge for these children, it is essential that you understand the progression in knowledge, skills and understanding within a unit of work so that you know what the 'next steps' in learning are. You must therefore research the progression sequence prior to teaching a unit of work.

To set tasks for pupils that are appropriate in their level of challenge, it is essential that you understand the progression in knowledge, skills and understanding within a unit of work.

Without this understanding, you will not be able to outline the 'next steps' in learning.

You must therefore research and understand the progression sequence prior to teaching a unit of work.

You will need to consider how you can support children who are working at lower stages of development by providing planned interventions and responsive same-day interventions to meet their needs. A child who is working at a higher stage of development in the area of mathematical calculations might be working at a lower stage of development within geometry. Therefore, it does not necessarily follow that a child who is weak at one aspect of a subject is weak at all aspects of that subject. This highlights the need for teachers to adopt flexible grouping arrangements and to avoid developing fixed mind-sets about children's abilities. Children may develop misconceptions within a lesson, but they may have demonstrated mastery of the content in the previous lesson. Same-day interventions provide an opportunity to address these misconceptions. Pre-teaching the lesson content prior to the taught lesson is also another useful way of giving children the best opportunity to make progress in the lesson.

## 1.5 SUPPORTING PUPILS FROM DISADVANTAGED BACKGROUNDS

The National Education Union (NEU) has produced a synthesis of key research. This is summarised below.

- Poverty is the strongest statistical predictor of how well a child will achieve at school.
- By Year 6, pupils living in poverty are often over nine months behind their peers in reading, writing and mathematics.
- The attainment gap widens for pupils throughout secondary school. Students eligible for free school meals are half as likely to achieve a good pass at General Certificate of Secondary Education (GCSE) in English and Mathematics in comparison to other students.
- Students living in poverty are four times more likely to be permanently excluded from school than their peers.
- Even with the same qualifications disadvantaged students are 50 per cent more likely to be Not in Education, Employment, or Training (NEET) after leaving school.
- Single parents are more likely to experience poverty than those families with both parents.
- People from Black and Ethnic Minority groups are also more likely to live in poverty.

(NEU, 2021)

It is important to recognise that pupils do not choose their social backgrounds and children's social backgrounds should not determine their aspirations. However, it is also important to be aware that social disadvantage can impact adversely on behavioural and emotional development, mental health, speech, language and communication and cognition. Pupils from areas of disadvantage can achieve well if they are taught by teachers who have high expectations of them and believe that they can achieve well. Schools should establish a culture of high expectations for all pupils because education provides them with an opportunity to break away from the cycle of disadvantage that may dominate their lives. It is particularly important that pupils from areas of social disadvantage have access to a broad and rich curriculum which provides them with the **cultural capital** that they need to succeed in life. Back in 2013, Michael Gove stated that 'The acquisition of cultural capital – the acquisition of [powerful] knowledge – is the key to social mobility'.

Some pupils might need additional resources and interventions to support them in their learning, particularly if they are deprived of books and technology at home. Schools can compensate for this disadvantage by ensuring that pupils have access to the resources they need to support their learning and by providing additional interventions to enable pupils to catch up and keep up with their peers.

## 1.6 FOSTERING EFFORT, CONCENTRATION AND PERSEVERANCE

Many children simply give up when they find specific subject content too difficult. However, with sustained effort, concentration and perseverance, they can improve their intelligence. You play a critical role in supporting children to recognise that intelligence is not a fixed trait. They need to understand that investing effort into a task is worthwhile because although the task may be difficult, effort, concentration and perseverance will eventually pay off and they will master it. Discussing things that you find difficult is one way of helping pupils realise that learning is not always straightforward. In fact, if it is meant to be difficult and if it is not difficult, then they are not being suitably challenged.

## 1.7 WORKING IN PARTNERSHIP WITH PARENTS

Developing effective professional relationships with parents is not always straightforward. Some parents will have unreasonable expectations of you and will attempt to place additional demands on you. Some will frustrate you because their expectations are too low. Some will not want to work with you because they have had negative experiences with teachers during their own education. It is important to keep an open mind. Some parents may be experiencing challenging personal circumstances that may impact their capacity to engage with you. Building relationships that are positive and underpinned by mutual respect may take some time. Informing them frequently of their child's successes is one way of establishing positive relationships. Smiling at them can work wonders; so, too, can demonstrating empathy through listening to them when they need to talk to you. Communicating with parents regularly through text messages, newsletters or the school website are also effective way of keeping parents informed.

## 1.8 CREATING A SAFE AND STIMULATING ENVIRONMENT

The primary classroom should provide a stimulating environment in which children can learn. Children need to be encouraged to respect their learning environment and they are more likely to do this if you also respect it. There should be a place for everything so that children know where to locate resources and storage facilities should be labelled so that children know where resources are kept. Avoid 'dumping' your resources in inappropriate places, and aim to be tidy and well-organised so that you know where to find things. There is nothing worse than finding a teacher's resources scattered on a tabletop display that is intended for children's use.

One organisational strategy that you might find useful is to organise your lesson resources into separate boxes or trays each day. Try to get these ready the previous day so that your lessons are prepared when you come to school. Try to devote dedicated time after school each day to preparing your resources for the next day. You can then quickly locate them between lessons, and this will help you to stay calm. You will find a system that ultimately works for you, but it is critical that you are organised. If you are not usually an organised person, now is the time to develop this important skill.

Encourage the children to take responsibility for their learning environment. They usually only do this when you communicate high expectations. Examples of 'non-negotiables' might include:

- A clear expectation that children will tidy their tables at the end of each lesson.
- An expectation that no resources or litter will be left on the floor at the end of each lesson or day.
- Coats in cloakrooms should be hung on pegs and not left lying around on the floor.
- Pencils, pens and rulers should be stored in the appropriate places.
- Chairs should be pushed under tables when children leave the classroom.

Assigning ownership of the learning environment to children will make your life easier, but it will also mean that the classroom is tidy and ready for the next lesson. These may seem like minor things that are not important. However, it is all part of what children need to learn and they should be given some ownership of their classroom. Allowing five minutes to tidy away at the end of each lesson will save you a lot of time. You will not have time to keep tidying the classroom between lessons, especially when you are getting your next lesson prepared.

The most stimulating primary classrooms are colourful, interesting and they promote a sense of curiosity. You will need to negotiate with your mentor how much ownership you can have of the learning environment, including displays, but you might find the following suggestions helpful.

- Create a stimulus display for your topic to engage children right from the start.
- Create interactive displays: create an investigation area to promote children's curiosity. For example, if the children are learning about electricity, you might place a collection of batteries, wires, bulbs, switches, motors and buzzers onto an investigation table. You might include some learning challenges for them to complete. In this instance, the challenge might include examples of different types of electrical circuits for the children to make. You might then include key questions – for example, 'How can you make the motor spin the opposite way?' You might want to include a large diagram of a circuit with key components labelled – for example, battery, bulb, wire and switch.
- Create working walls for mathematics and English. These could be changed when you move on to a new unit of work. On the working wall you could include key vocabulary that the children need to learn, worked examples, manipulative mathematical resources and samples of children's work. In English, the working wall could be created as pupils work through a unit of work to demonstrate the complete writing process – i.e. stimulus, vocabulary generation, planning, drafting, redrafting and the final product.
- Create displays of children's work to celebrate their amazing achievements. Make sure that children's names are included next to the work. Also display photographs to illustrate the learning process as well as the products of learning – for example, capturing moments when children are working on collaborative tasks.
- Create a stimulating reading area that includes texts related to the topics that children are studying.
- Create a display of the text that the children are studying in English.

You should expect children to show respect to you, each other and to their learning environment. If your expectations are too low, these will be reflected in their behaviour. Young children learn very quickly what your expectations are. They may test you initially, but when they realise that your expectations will not alter, they usually comply.

You must make sure that the classroom is a safe place for children to learn by removing resources or equipment that might be dangerous. If the school hall is used as a dining room, but also used for physical education, it is worth checking that it is fit to use before you take children in, especially if the policy is for children not to use footwear. Although this might feel like a menial job, it is important to protect children from accidents.

### TAKE 5

- Use open questions to promote cognitive demand.
- Scaffold questioning to ensure that pupils cannot opt-out.
- Have routines and procedures in place that support pupils to manage themselves.
- Insist that pupils use precise, technical vocabulary.
- Communicate regularly with parents in order to establish positive relationships.

## CLASSROOM EXAMPLE

It is important to support pupils to provide the right or valid answers to any questions that they are asked. When pupil responses include 'I'm not sure' or 'I don't know', it is essential that action is taken to develop confidence and understanding. In these cases, you should adapt your approach to questioning to ensure that the sequence ends with the pupil providing a right or valid answer to the question that you initially posed. It may be appropriate to ask the question in a different way, or to model the answer and ask the pupil to repeat it after you. You may also find it helpful to ask another pupil the question and then ask the initial pupil to repeat the answer. In some cases, it may be possible to deconstruct the question and in doing so 'chunk' the content that you are discussing to enable the pupil to find the answer. Similarly, other pupils can be called upon to provide cues and prompts, and the initial pupil can then use these to find the answer to the question that you originally posed. These questioning approaches ensure the highest expectations of pupil involvement as it significantly reduces their ability to opt out of your questioning.

## EXAMPLES OF WHAT GOOD PRACTICE IN HIGH EXPECTATIONS LOOKS LIKE IN THE CLASSROOM

Plan your lesson to build on pupils' existing knowledge and skills. Your assessments of children's learning will determine your starting point for planning lessons. Include plenty of questions that promote thinking during the lesson and plan for these in advance. Include challenge tasks for those children who need additional cognitive demands during the lesson. Plan for pupils working at lower levels of development to achieve the same learning outcomes as other pupils by breaking tasks down further or by providing additional adult support and resources to support them. Do not automatically set them a less challenging task unless the learning outcomes that have been set for other pupils are not developmentally suitable for pupils operating at lower stages of development.

## SUMMARY

This chapter has outlined the importance of setting high expectations for all pupils and it has highlighted how teachers' beliefs can have a substantial impact on pupil learning. Having high expectations is essential in order to ensure that all pupils are exposed to cognitively demanding experiences and advanced learning opportunities. The chapter has also explained why it is important to ensure that you demonstrate the highest standards of your own professional behaviour, and it has indicated your roles and responsibilities as a role model. Practical guidance has been offered to support your own professional practice and a range of strategies have been discussed in relation to pedagogical approaches to support challenge and participation. The chapter has also provided some practical examples of effective classroom practice and a selection of takeaways to support your teaching.

# 2

# HOW PUPILS LEARN

## IN THIS CHAPTER

Classrooms are dynamic environments in which teachers, pupils and learning materials all interact with one another. Learning occurs best when pupils develop positive attitudes and perceptions as part of the learning experience. Within this chapter, key research is outlined to support you in reflecting the factors that contribute to learning. As a trainee teacher, you are accountable for pupils' attainment and progress within lessons and across sequences of lessons. Practical guidance is offered to support you in facilitating pupil progress, and we have outlined the characteristics of what constitutes effective practice over time. To support your understanding of the learning process, we have outlined existing research and evidence-based strategies relating to memory, schemas, chunking, misconceptions and retrieval. A range of work examples and takeaways are provided to support you in the classroom.

## KEY RESEARCH

The evidence from research has demonstrated the following:

- *Children's learning and development are shaped by a combination of environmental factors and learning opportunities both inside and outside schools.*
- *Learning involves physical, psychological, social and emotional processes. These influence one another in that the interactions between these processes can enable or restrict learning.*
- *The brain and intelligence are malleable and can be changed by environmental influences, including exposure to high-quality teaching.*
- *Our experiences activate neural pathways that enable new ways of thinking and new skills to develop.*

- *Emotions and social contexts shape neural connections which contribute to attention, concentration and memory as well as knowledge transfer and application. Research has demonstrated that chronic stress due to trauma affects cognition and working memory.*
- *Differentiated instruction enables optimum brain growth.*

(Wei et al., 2019)

- *According to* Sweller et al. (2011), *'if nothing in the long-term memory has been altered, nothing has been learned'. Research suggests that an effective approach to curriculum planning is to repeat practice over time, as this leads to better long-term retention of knowledge (*Rawson and Kintsch, 2005*). This is known as spaced or distributed practice. Reviewing previous learning leads to much greater long-term retention if subject content is spread out, with gaps in between to allow students to forget the content (*Coe et al., 2014*). This 'is one of the most general and robust effects from across the entire history of experimental research on learning and memory'* (Bjork and Bjork, 2011, p59). *Many students benefit from repeated exposure to subject content, particularly when content is spaced out and revisited rather than taught in a single block and never revisited.*

## KEY POLICY

The *Teachers' Standards* state that teachers must:

- *be accountable for pupils' attainment, progress and outcomes.*
- *be aware of pupils' capabilities and their prior knowledge, and plan teaching to build on these.*
- *guide pupils to reflect on the progress they have made and their emerging needs.*
- *demonstrate knowledge and understanding of how pupils learn and how this impacts on teaching.*
- *encourage pupils to take a responsible and conscientious attitude to their own work and study.*

(DfE, 2011)

## 2.1 BEING ACCOUNTABLE FOR PUPILS' ATTAINMENT AND PROGRESS

As a trainee teacher, you are accountable for the progress of the children you teach both within individual lessons and across a sequence of lessons. You will need to know the starting points of your children at the beginning of a teaching placement. You can then assess them at the end of the placement to determine whether they have made adequate progress. You will need to be able to explain the reasons why some children have made less than expected progress and you should also plan subject-specific interventions during your placement to enable those children who are making insufficient progress to move forward in their learning.

One way of ensuring progress within lessons is to plan lessons with a clear structure that supports progress. There are various ways of facilitating progress within lessons and these are outlined below:

- Organise the aspects of knowledge or skills sequentially and teach the relevant content in the correct order across a sequence of lessons.
- Build in sufficient opportunities for children to practise and apply the knowledge and skills they are taught.
- Provide children with opportunities to consolidate their learning to enable them to develop fluency.
- Model multiple examples of the subject content and check that they understand it.

It is important that children make progress across a sequence of lessons. In order to secure progress, you will need to become skilled at planning lesson sequences that enable children to make progress over time. Effective planning should ensure that *over time* children develop:

- Greater knowledge
- An increased understanding of the subject content
- Greater proficiency in applying their knowledge and skills in different contexts
- Greater confidence in the subject content
- Greater fluency in the subject
- Good attitudes to learning in relation to the subject content
- Higher quality work in children's books
- Greater productivity in their work
- Increased resilience when they are faced with challenging tasks

All of these are measures of progress. Thus, progress does not always need to be measured through test scores and grades. If children become more confident in applying a mathematical skill to solve mathematical word problems presented in different ways, increased confidence and fluency in completing this task is an indication that they have made progress.

On a weekly basis, during mentor meetings, you should be prepared to discuss which children have made insufficient progress in your lessons and the actions you intend to take to address this. You should not leave consideration of children's progress until you have completed a unit of work, or even completed your placement. Reflecting on the progress of your children regularly throughout your placement will ensure that you can implement swift interventions to accelerate their progress.

When you evaluate your teaching, you should reflect carefully on which children made good progress and those who made progress that was less than expected both in lessons and across sequences of lessons. By identifying these children immediately, you can adapt subsequent lessons or plan interventions to help them overcome barriers to learning and misconceptions.

## 2.2 HOW CHILDREN LEARN

Learning involves an alteration in long-term memory. Learning involves a lasting change in pupils' capabilities or understanding. Pupils make progress when they know more, remember more and can do more within subjects. Pupils need to learn foundational knowledge before they can process more complex subject content. For example, in early reading, they need to know the phonemes representing specific graphemes before they can meaningfully start to blend phonemes for word recognition. They need to learn a simple alphabetic code before they learn a complex alphabetic code. In mathematics, pupils need to learn informal methods for solving the four operations before progressing to formal methods. Committing some key facts to memory will help pupils to learn more complex ideas. For example, if pupils learn number pairs that make 10, they can easily learn to identify pairs of numbers that make 100 or 1,000. If they develop mathematical fluency with multiplication facts, they can subsequently use these to solve mathematical word problems.

Research demonstrates that:

> *Experience is a 'stressor' to brain growth—throughout life, interpersonal experiences and relational connections activate neural pathways, generating energy flow through electrical impulses that strengthen connectivity.*
>
> (Cantor et al., 2019, p311)

A combination of both genetic factors and early experiences shapes neuronal connections that develop neural circuits. These enable increasingly complex mental activities to occur (Moore, 2015; Slavich and Cole, 2013). As these circuits become increasingly stable, they contribute to the development of complex thoughts, skills and behaviours in individuals (Cantor et al., 2019). Environmental and interpersonal experiences influence brain growth throughout childhood and well into adulthood. It has been demonstrated that *genes act as followers, not prime movers, in developmental processes* (Cantor et al., 2019, p309). It has also been demonstrated that positive, nurturing relationships are essential to brain development. These relationships build strong brain architecture (Cantor et al., 2019). We know that children's development is shaped by micro-ecological contexts (i.e. families, peers, schools and communities) as well as macro-ecological contexts (i.e. economic and cultural systems).

The brain is characterised by plasticity rather than stability. Its structure is influenced not just by genetics, but by the micro and macro contexts within which individuals are situated. Physical, psychological, social and emotional processes also influence brain structure. Emotions can have powerful effects on developmental pathways (Cantor et al., 2019). The implications of this are significant because the research demonstrates that an individual's experiences can shape the development of neural pathways which facilitate mental processes. Thus, exposure to high-quality teaching can change the structure of the brain by activating new neural pathways.

## 2.3 MEMORY

An important factor in learning is memory. Memory comprises two elements: the working memory and the long-term memory.

- The working memory holds a limited amount of information. The working memory is where information that is actively processed is held. The capacity of the working memory is limited, and it can quickly become overloaded.
- The long-term memory stores information indefinitely, including information which is not being used in the short-term memory. It is a store of knowledge that changes as pupils learn more. Regular purposeful practice of what has been previously taught can help consolidate material and help pupils remember what they have learned. Repetition and practice are required to 'fix' information in the long-term memory, but once it is stored in the long-term memory it can remain there indefinitely.

### WORKING MEMORY

When new subject content is introduced to pupils in lessons, the working memory processes that information. The processing of subject content takes place in the working memory. The working memory can only process a limited amount of information. Once information has been processed it then transfers to the long-term memory where it is stored. The working memory is made up of several components. These are shown in Figure 2.1.

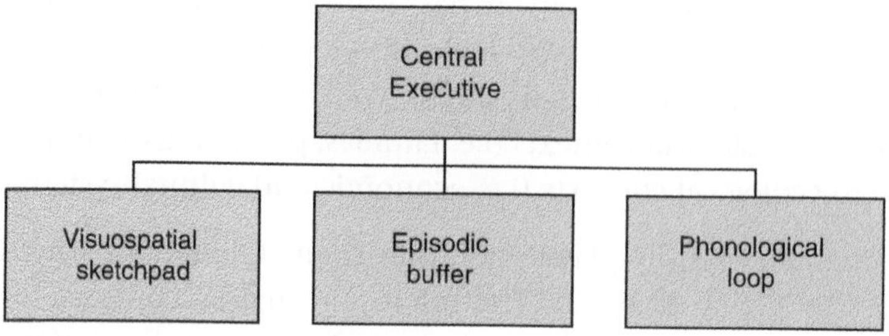


**Figure 2.1** Model of the working memory

The working memory is a multi-component system made up of different parts, The central executive drives the working memory, although there is little direct evidence for how the central executive works. It allocates information to the phonological loop and the visuospatial sketchpad. These are processing chambers. The central executive therefore plays a role in deciding which chamber to send information to for processing. The visuospatial sketchpad is the component of the working memory that stores and processes visual and spatial information. For example, when children are actively processing a photograph or a diagram, the visuospatial sketchpad will actively process that visual information. Navigation tasks are also processed in this component of the working memory. The phonological loop is the component of the working memory that processes spoken and written information, including processing sounds of speech and vocabulary. Reading is a task that is processed in the phonological loop. The episodic buffer was added to the model of the working memory in the year 2000. It acts as a 'back-up' store which communicates with the long-term memory and the components of the working memory.

## PURPOSEFUL PRACTICE

Regular purposeful practice can help pupils to remember what they have learned. In a lesson, it is therefore beneficial to provide pupils with tasks so that they can practice the subject content. Think about the task of learning to drive a car. The driving instructor instructs the learner driver how to perform specific tasks associated with driving, but the learner driver will only master the tasks to automaticity through regular purposeful practice. Once automaticity has been achieved, this limits the load on the working memory. Table 2.1 shows an example of how this might look in practice.

**Table 2.1** Example of spaced or distributed practice

| | **Content (Science example)** |
|---|---|
| **Autumn 1** | Plants - 4 weeks<br>Forces - 3 weeks |
| **Autumn 2** | Electricity - 6 weeks |
| **Spring 1** | Materials - 6 weeks |
| **Spring 2** | Forces - 4 weeks |
| **Summer 1** | Plants - 6 weeks |
| **Summer 2** | Electricity - 5 weeks<br>Materials - 5 weeks |

The basic idea is that content is revisited after a gap so that pupils almost forget what they have learned. Pupils are required to retrieve the prior knowledge from their long-term memory. Teachers then build on the existing knowledge to enable pupils to form more complex schemas.

## LONG-TERM MEMORY

The long-term memory takes information from the working memory and stores it. Theoretically, it has an unlimited capacity, although some information may be less accessible. It is divided into two types: explicit (knowing that) and implicit (knowing how).

- Explicit (declarative) long-term memory includes episodic memory and semantic memory. Episodic memory is the part of the explicit long-term memory that is responsible for storing information about events that we have experienced. It helps us to remember our first day at school or a childhood holiday. Semantic memory is a part of the explicit long-term memory that is responsible for storing knowledge about the world, for example, knowledge of capital cities or knowledge of the meanings of words.
- Implicit (non-declarative) long-term memory includes procedural memory which is the part of the long-term memory that stores information about how to do things, for example, knowledge of how to ride a bicycle. It also includes emotional memory (affective memory) which includes memory of experiences that may have triggered emotional reactions.

### THE IMPORTANCE OF MEMORY IN THE PROCESS OF LEARNING

As a teacher, it is important to limit the amount of information that you ask pupils to process at any one time. The capacity of the working memory is limited and breaking content down into manageable chunks limits the load on the working memory. Information that has been processed in the working memory then transfers to long-term memory where it is stored. The long-term memory organises different types of information into categories, acting rather like a filing cabinet. Information sharing similar characteristics is grouped and stored. However, if information is never retrieved from long-term memory, it is likely that it will be forgotten. Requiring pupils to retrieve information after it has been stored in their long-term memory is an effective way of strengthening recall.

### SPACED OR DISTRIBUTED PRACTICE

Spaced or distributed practice is the practice of spacing out curriculum content over time so that content is revisited. Teachers can use this as an opportunity to check that pupils' knowledge of content is secure before deepening their knowledge of that content.

## 2.4 COGNITIVE LOAD

Pupils experience cognitive load when too much information is channelled into a specific component of the working memory. This prevents the working memory from working efficiently and pupils cannot process the subject content. There are three main types of cognitive load:

- Intrinsic load: This occurs when pupils are given too much information, even though it may all be relevant. The working memory becomes overloaded, and this reduces its efficiency. Intrinsic load should therefore be reduced by limiting the amount of information that pupils are required to focus on in any lesson.
- Extraneous load: This occurs when pupils are asked to process additional content which is not essential to the core learning. The extraneous content overloads the working memory and the core knowledge that pupils need to learn is not processed and therefore not understood. Extraneous load should therefore be reduced in lessons.
- Germane load: this occurs when a schema is modified, resulting in a more complex schema forming. This results in deep and transformative learning and therefore this type of load should be increased.

> THE BRAIN IS …
> characterised by plasticity rather than stability.
> The structure of the brain is influenced not just by genetics but by: the MICRO contexts (families, peers, schools and communities) and MACRO contexts (economic and cultural systems) within which individuals are situated.
>
> (Cantor et al., 2019)

## 2.5 ACTIVATING PRIOR KNOWLEDGE: SCHEMAS

Pupils make progress when more complex schemas develop. One of the ways through which the brain stores information is the development of schemas. Schemas are mental structures of frameworks for representing some aspect of the world, including knowledge. Organising knowledge into schemas facilitates its retrieval from long-term memory. Schemas can be considered to be categories that a child develops through their interactions with the world and with others – for example, a child may develop a schema about dogs. They learn that dogs have four legs and a tail, and they apply this schema to identify dogs when they see one. Initially, they may see a specific dog type (e.g., a Labrador), and they learn that the category of 'dog' applies to this animal. After this, they see a wider variety of dog breeds but because they all have four legs and a tail, they learn that the category of 'dog' does not just apply to Labradors. This is new learning, but the schema does not need to be modified. After a while see a wider variety of animals with four legs and a tail (cats, lions and horses), and they may assume these are dogs, but they learn that different categories apply to these animals and due to this the schema needs to be modified, i.e., an animal with four legs and a tail may be a cat, a horse or a lion.

Schemas continue to develop throughout childhood and into adult life. They are convenient categories for storing information to aid retrieval. One way of thinking about them is to imagine that they are storage folders that group together information that will fit into a specific category. Initially, pupils associate the grapheme 'ch' with the sound they can hear at the beginning of the following words: chip, chair, church, cheese and chicken. They form a schema or mental representation for the grapheme 'ch'. Later in their reading development, they progress from learning a simple alphabetic code to a complex code. They learn that the grapheme 'ch' can represent the phoneme /sh/ in 'chef' and /k/ in the chemist. The schema for the grapheme 'ch', therefore, becomes more complex, and it is extended from a simple representation of the grapheme 'ch' to a more complex representation as shown in Figures 2.2 and 2.3.

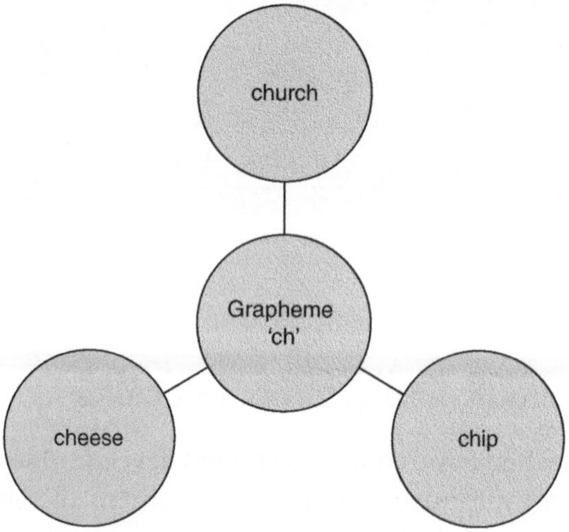


**Figure 2.2** Simple Schema for the grapheme 'ch'

Piaget (1896–1980) articulated how new learning occurs using schemas. He used the term 'assimilation' when new information is added to current schemas. In the example above, the child's existing schema – i.e., that a dog has four legs and a tail – is

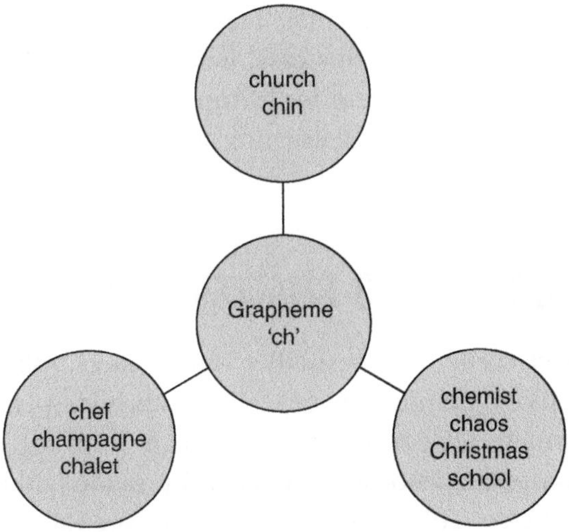


**Figure 2.3** Complex Schema for grapheme 'ch'

applied to different sizes, colours and breeds of dog. The schema still works because the animals are all dogs. Piaget referred to this as a process of 'equilibrium'. However, 'disequilibrium' occurs when new information cannot be fitted into existing schemas. This causes the child to experience what Piaget referred to as 'cognitive dissonance'. This is where schemas are forced to change to 'accommodate' new information. This happens when the existing schema (knowledge) does not work and needs to be changed to deal with a new object or situation. In the same example, the child may see a horse and call it a dog, but then subsequently learns that this is incorrect. The schema no longer works and needs to be changed. The process of reframing a schema can be challenging, but this is when learning occurs. It is the process through which new knowledge is accommodated with existing knowledge to return to a state of equilibrium. The processes of equilibrium and disequilibrium then continue as schemas become increasingly more complex.

When you activate pupils' prior knowledge, you are activating the schema which they have already formed. You will need to remind the pupils about their prior learning. Through using specific assessment strategies, such as questioning, you will be able to ascertain whether they have retained prior subject content in the long-term memory. As you introduce new subject content, the pupils will need to accommodate the new information within the existing schema, which subsequently changes the schema. As they experience disequilibrium, they might find the new learning difficult. This is all part of the learning process. New learning is difficult, and you will need to encourage your pupils to invest effort and perseverance at this stage.

When activating prior learning, you may realise that existing knowledge, understanding or skills are not secure. In this case, before you ask them to accommodate new learning, you need to revisit the prior learning to address their misconceptions. If you do not do this, the subsequent learning will not have secure foundations to become secure.

## 2.6 BREAKING CONTENT INTO SMALLER STEPS

Breaking down subject content into smaller bite-sized chunks or into a series of smaller sequential steps is a helpful way of scaffolding children's understanding. This process is called chunking. It reduces the load on the working memory. It is often helpful to model each of the associated steps and provide children with an opportunity to practise each step. This enables you to integrate formative assessment into your teaching because through creating opportunities for pupils to practise each step, you are then able to assess their understanding of the subject content at each stage of the lesson and address misconceptions before you move on to the next step.

It is also useful to write the steps down and give these to the pupils so that they have a visual reminder of the steps they need to do to achieve success in the task. In addition, some teachers accompany each step with a worked example so that pupils can see what they need to do at each stage during the task.

## 2.7 ADDRESSING MISCONCEPTIONS

Developing misconceptions is a normal part of the learning process. Your role as a teacher is to notice and respond to misconceptions in lessons. This will enable your pupils to make further progress. Strategies for addressing misconceptions are outlined below:

- Modelling misconceptions to pupils by making deliberate errors and drawing their attention to these
- Highlighting common misconceptions to children when you model new subject content to prevent them from making the same mistakes
- Building assessment tasks or questions into lessons to identify specific children who have developed misconceptions
- Noticing misconceptions occurring as pupils work on tasks and then subsequently providing focused support to address these misconceptions directly

- Using pre-teaching to address misconceptions with specific pupils
- Providing post-lesson interventions to address misconceptions
- Sharing examples of children's work and highlighting misconceptions
- Asking pupils to highlight errors on a piece of work
- Using peer–peer support to address misconceptions

## 2.8 RETRIEVAL

Asking pupils to retrieve information that you have previously taught them during lessons, across sequences of lessons and across a school year is an effective way of activating prior knowledge which is stored in long-term memory. Retrieval practice strengthens memory and aids long-term retention (Barenberg et al., 2018; Roediger and Karpicke, 2006). Examples of pedagogical approaches that can be used for retrieval practice include:

- Tests and quizzes
- Making lists
- Adding labels to a diagram
- Questioning
- Asking pupils to summarise their understanding of subject content that has previously been taught
- Asking pupils to work in pairs on a question they have practised before
- Planning a group collaborative activity which activates prior learning
- Using software packages that provide activities based on prior learning

## 2.9 HOW PUPILS LEARN MATHEMATICS

In the early stages of learning mathematics, many children require the use of manipulatives to support them in developing their understanding of mathematical concepts. Effective modelling of mathematical concepts and skills will support children in developing mathematical understanding. Providing children with opportunities to revisit learning to consolidate their understanding will support them in developing mathematical fluency. Children need frequent opportunities to develop their skills in mental mathematics and they can learn specific mental calculation strategies to support them with mental arithmetic. Children require frequent opportunities to practise the mathematical skills they have been taught. In addition, they need to apply their mathematical skills to real-life problems, and they need to be able to develop fluency in applying subject content in different contexts. This will help them to develop mathematical mastery.

## 2.10 HOW PUPILS LEARN ENGLISH

English includes spoken language, reading and writing. Although these skills should be developed within the context of English lessons, children need to apply these skills across the curriculum to the same standard that they use in English. Spoken language, reading and writing are all interrelated and should not be viewed as distinct aspects. Pupils need to be taught a rich and challenging vocabulary. They need to be introduced to texts that excite, motivate and challenge them. They need to develop a love of reading and writing from inspirational teachers who are themselves avid readers and writers. They need to be taught the skills that underpin reading and writing, but essentially children need to be supported to apply these skills to reading and writing. Phonics is only a useful tool if children use it to support their reading and writing. Children can learn about the adjective in grammar, but it is only useful if children apply this knowledge to their writing.

Drama is a powerful tool to excite and motivate children, but it is also an excellent vehicle for developing spoken language. In addition, it can provide children with rich immersive experiences that enable them to produce richer writing.

Developing pupils' knowledge of grammar and phonics is crucial but so too is developing within pupils a love for reading and writing. Reading powerful literature with the whole class from key children's authors can help foster a love of reading. Bringing poets, authors and other creative artists into the classroom to work with pupils can foster a love of drama, debate, reading and writing. Visiting theatres and libraries can provide children with forms of cultural capital that they may be missing at home. Being taught by a teacher who is also a reader can be extremely motivating, particularly when teachers start to share the texts they are reading with their pupils. Writing alongside children in the classroom is also an effective strategy because it elevates the status of writing. Writing collaboratively with children and providing opportunities for children to collaborate on a piece of writing are also very effective strategies.

## 2.11 HOW PUPILS LEARN IN THE WIDER CURRICULUM

The wider curriculum in primary school is often referred to as the foundation subjects. However, the problem with this phrase is that it leads to the assumption that these subjects are less important. All subjects are important. Providing children with a broad curriculum enables them to identify what they are good at across a broad range of subjects.

Children need rich opportunities to learn through investigation by engaging in enquiry-based learning. This is critical not only in science but also in other subjects such as history and geography. In these subjects, children learn to interact with a range of primary and secondary source materials (including site visits) to discover the geography of their school or local area, or to find out about what life was like in the past. In religious education, children learn about the beliefs of others through a process of investigative enquiry in which they explore religions through photographs, artefacts, site visits and opportunities to listen to religious leaders.

Children need opportunities to learn skills in art and design and technology, and then to apply these by producing creations and making products. We believe that all children in primary school should learn to play a musical instrument. In physical education, children learn the benefits of physical activity and learn to participate in team and individual sports. These are illustrative examples that highlight the importance of learning through first-hand experiences.

## 2.12 DEVELOPING METACOGNITION

Metacognition is the skill of learning how to learn. You can support the development of children's metacognitive skills by providing them with clear checklists of aspects that will make their work successful. These are often referred to as success criteria. As they complete a task, they can use the checklists to monitor and evaluate their own learning. This is only one example of a metacognitive strategy. You can also support the children to reflect on the strengths and weaknesses of their work and themselves as a learner in general. This ability to reflect on oneself and identify areas for improvement is a vital metacognitive skill because it promotes future growth.

## 2.13 WORKED EXAMPLES

Worked examples are particularly powerful in promoting learning gains for pupils. Worked examples can include the following:

- Examples of writing
- Examples of how to complete a worksheet
- Models of the steps to follow through a problem – for example, the steps through a mathematical problem

- Examples of finished products – for example, in design and technology
- Examples of good answers to examination questions

Teachers can use dialogue to explain the salient features of the worked example. This enables them to emphasise the aspects that make it effective. Teachers can also use dialogue to model a worked example. They might model the process of completing a mathematical calculation, constructing a piece of writing, conducting a scientific investigation.

### TAKE 5

- Use worked examples to promote pupils' learning.
- Use regular testing and quizzing to support pupils' retrieval.
- Make deliberate errors to draw pupils' attention to misconceptions.
- Plan specific opportunities to remind pupils about their prior learning.
- Break down subject content to scaffold pupils' understanding.

## CLASSROOM EXAMPLE

In English, model the writing process. Model the process of thinking out loud and making decisions about what content to include in the writing. Model specifically the process of orally rehearsing writing, using 'think it', 'say it', 'write it' and 'read it' for all sentences. Say your sentences out loud. Model the language features and structural conventions of the genre. Develop a good level of subject knowledge so that you know what grammatical, vocabulary and punctuation features you need to model in the writing so that children have access to a high-quality model of writing that aligns with age-related expectations in the national curriculum.

## EXAMPLES OF WHAT GOOD PRACTICE IN MATHS LOOKS LIKE IN THE CLASSROOM

- Limit the amount of content that you introduce in lessons.
- Build retrieval tasks into lessons to activate knowledge that is stored in the long-term memory.
- Use manipulatives in mathematics to develop pupils' understanding of mathematical concepts.

- Revisit subject content after a gap by spacing out and revisiting subject content.
- Allow pupils to experiment with a range of different learning opportunities so that they experience concepts using concrete resources, and visual and mental strategies.
- Revisit the concept using pencil and paper strategies, and draw on the range of activities to activate pupils' prior learning.

## SUMMARY

This chapter has highlighted teachers' roles and responsibilities in relation to how pupils learn. In doing so, it has outlined the characteristics of effective practice including retrieval practice, spaced or distributed practice and worked examples. The role of working memory and long-term memory in the process of learning has also been discussed. Throughout the chapter, we have encouraged you to reflect on the factors that support pupil learning and the implications of these for your own practice. We have also outlined barriers and enablers to good progress, and guidance has been offered to support you to address these within your own classroom.

# 3

# SUBJECT AND CURRICULUM

## IN THIS CHAPTER

Subject knowledge for teaching extends beyond the ability to demonstrate strong knowledge and understanding of subject content. Teachers must also demonstrate a secure understanding of how to communicate effectively the subject content to pupils and a good understanding of children's development. Some subjects such as mathematics and English may be taught separately. However, other subjects, particularly the foundation subjects, may be taught using a cross-curricular approach in which subjects are taught through themes or topics. It is important that children have access to a broad, rich and balanced curriculum throughout their primary education. It is also essential that children are provided with opportunities to apply their subject-specific learning in mathematics and English in the foundation subjects. It is also critical that even when subjects are taught using a cross-curricular approach, the subject-specific knowledge, concepts and skills are not diluted. Effective primary school teachers require a broad body of knowledge to teach across a range of subjects.

It is not practical to cover all aspects of subject and curriculum knowledge, and this chapter does not attempt to do so. Instead, it outlines key research to support your understanding of over-arching concepts, including subject-specific knowledge and skills. It also offers practical strategies to foster pupils' subject interests and to enable you to identify and address subject-specific misconceptions.

## KEY RESEARCH

According to Coe et al.:

> *The most effective teachers have deep knowledge of the subjects they teach, and when teachers' knowledge falls below a certain level it is a significant impediment to students' learning. As well as a strong understanding of the material being taught, teachers must also understand the ways students think about the content, be able to*

*evaluate the thinking behind students' own methods and identify students' common misconceptions.*

(Coe et al., 2014, p2)

## KEY POLICY

The *Teachers' Standards* state that teachers must:

- *have a secure knowledge of the relevant subject(s) and curriculum areas, foster and maintain pupils' interest in the subject, and address misunderstandings.*
- *demonstrate a critical understanding of developments in the subject and curriculum areas, and promote the value of scholarship.*
- *demonstrate an understanding of and take responsibility for promoting high standards of literacy, articulacy and the correct use of standard English, whatever the teacher's specialist subjects.*
- *if teaching early reading, demonstrate a clear understanding of systematic synthetic phonics.*
- *if teaching early mathematics, demonstrate a clear understanding of appropriate teaching strategies.*

(DfE, 2011)

## 3.1 SUBJECT-SPECIFIC KNOWLEDGE AND SKILLS

Your subject knowledge for teaching is made up of the following aspects:

- Subject knowledge per se: this is your knowledge of the subject content – its concepts, facts, theories and skills.
- Knowledge of pupils' development.
- Pedagogical knowledge.

Your knowledge of the subject content is critical to effective teaching and outcomes for children. Strong subject knowledge will give you the confidence to explain things clearly, to answer children's questions and to address their misconceptions. Having a strong grasp of the subject content will also enable you to provide suitable learning challenges for children who are operating at higher stages of development.

Making decisions about how to sequence subject content across a sequence of lessons requires you to understand how knowledge, skills and understanding progress across a unit of work. Having a secure knowledge of subject progression will enable you to address misconceptions and challenge children further.

Ofsted categorises subject knowledge into content knowledge, pedagogical knowledge and pedagogical content knowledge.

- **Content knowledge** is teachers' knowledge of the subject they are teaching.
- **Pedagogical knowledge** is teachers' knowledge of effective teaching methods.
- **Pedagogical content knowledge** is teachers' knowledge of how to teach the subject or topic.

(Ofsted, 2019b, p10)

## 3.2 OFSTED CURRICULUM RESEARCH REVIEWS

The Ofsted curriculum research reviews can be found using the following link:

https://www.gov.uk/government/collections/curriculum-research-reviews

It is essential that teachers read these because they outline the different types of subject knowledge in each subject. The type of subject knowledge varies from subject to subject, but the reports outline what pupil progress looks like in each subject.

## 3.3 SUBSTANTIVE KNOWLEDGE

Substantive knowledge relates to the subject concepts, facts and principles. It forms the substance of each subject. In history, there are specific subject concepts that pupils need to know and remember. These include knowledge of empire, parliament, democracy, trade and the military. This is not an exhaustive list. Pupils need to learn the dates of significant events and understand the difference between past and present. In science, pupils need to learn about the parts of the flowering plant, the circulatory system and the meanings of terms such as herbivore, omnivore and carnivore. In music, pupils need to know what 'pitch' means. These are examples of substantive knowledge. Pupils can learn substantive knowledge through different pedagogical approaches, but explicit, direct teaching plays an important role in developing pupils' substantive knowledge. It is important that pupils learn the correct knowledge from the teacher and pupils should not simply be left to discover that knowledge by themselves.

## 3.4 DISCIPLINARY KNOWLEDGE

Disciplinary knowledge refers to knowledge of how subject experts work within a subject. In science, discoveries are made by scientists working scientifically. Scientists generate hypotheses, design investigations or experiments, control variables, collect measurements and record results, evaluate the evidence and draw conclusions. The process of working scientifically is the disciplinary knowledge that pupils need to develop. Historians evaluate source material, compare sources, detect bias and they piece together different types of historical information. The knowledge of how historians work is disciplinary knowledge.

## 3.5 EXAMPLES OF SUBJECT KNOWLEDGE IN MATHEMATICS

The Ofsted curriculum research reports outline the different types of subject knowledge in mathematics. These are summarised below:

- **Declarative knowledge:** 'I know that'. This includes knowledge of mathematical facts and concepts.
- **Procedural knowledge:** 'I know how'. This includes knowledge of mathematical procedures.
- **Conditional knowledge:** 'I know when'. This includes mathematical reasoning, for example, explaining when to use a specific mathematical operation.

(Ofsted, 2021b)

## 3.6 PEDAGOGICAL SUBJECT KNOWLEDGE

Knowing a subject and understanding the steps that pupils need to learn the subject content are not enough in themselves. You also need to develop your knowledge of how to teach that subject content to enable pupils to learn it. Children learn initially through concrete representations before progressing to abstract representations and abstract thinking. Young children may require access to manipulative objects and visual forms of representations to support them in their learning. Examples in mathematics include the use of counters, place-value apparatus, cubes, money and small clocks for learning time. Children may also need access to number lines, number squares and multiplication tables.

In history, young children learn more effectively when they can explore historical artefacts as part of historical enquiry. The concept of chronology needs to be

# SUBJECT KNOWLEDGE MATTERS

Your knowledge of the subject content is critical to effective teaching and outcomes for children.

Strong subject knowledge will give you confidence to explain things clearly, to answer children's questions and to address their misconceptions.

Having a strong grasp of the subject content will also enable you to provide suitable learning challenges for children who are operating at higher stages of development.

developed from the child's own chronology before progressing to more abstract timelines. In geography, children need to learn about the geography of their school and locality before progressing on to learning about the geography of the wider world. It is always more effective to start from children's own experiences before progressing away from these. In science, children learn about scientific concepts and scientific facts by working scientifically through the exploration of practical first-hand experiences. Young children learn to be mathematicians, writers, scientists, historians, geographers and artists by *experiencing* the subject in a very active way.

Knowing how to sequence the subject-specific knowledge and skills is an essential aspect of your pedagogical subject knowledge. Correct sequencing of subject content enables pupils to make sense of a subject because lesson content logically builds on content that pupils have already been taught. The ability to logically sequence subject content will enable you to support the progress of your learners.

Identifying pupils' misconceptions is addressed later in this chapter. The ability to unpick subject-specific misconceptions helps you to understand how they have occurred in the first place. Effective teachers address these as they occur but also research common misconceptions when they are planning lessons. Knowing the common misconceptions is useful because you can then highlight these explicitly to children when you are introducing them to the subject content.

Understanding how to structure subject content across sequences of lessons so that pupils commit it to their long-term memory is also an aspect of pedagogical subject knowledge. Pupils are more likely to retain subject knowledge and skills if there are opportunities for them to revisit content over the year and build on what they already know and can do. Spacing learning out over time rather than teaching it in a single block is a more effective way of aiding long-term retention of subject content.

## 3.7 FOSTERING PUPILS' INTEREST IN YOUR SUBJECT

Securing children's interest in a subject emerges from being exposed to teachers who are enthusiastic, interesting and passionate about what they are teaching. The best teachers can even make very 'dry' content interesting. The following strategies should support you in fostering pupils' interest in subject content:

- Plan a 'hook' at the start of the lesson to get their attention (see Chapter 4)
- Break up the lesson into a series of cumulative stages, setting short, sharp and snappy tasks for children at each stage
- Provide frequent opportunities for active learning and for children to learn through first-hand experiences

- Provide opportunities for children to work in pairs
- Provide opportunities for children to work in small groups
- Provide opportunities to develop oracy through all subjects
- Use drama as a pedagogical tool where this is appropriate

## 3.8 SUBJECT-SPECIFIC MISCONCEPTIONS

Children may develop misconceptions about specific aspects of the subject content. Your role as a teacher is to unpick these misconceptions with them, explain to them why these have developed, and support them to develop accurate knowledge and understanding.

The best way of addressing misconceptions is to research possible misconceptions that children may develop when you are planning lessons. This will then enable you to highlight explicitly these common misconceptions in your lesson, thus drawing attention to them, and teaching children to avoid developing them in the first place.

Understanding common misconceptions within a subject and supporting pupils to overcome these requires you to have strong subject knowledge. You will also need to ensure that you do not accidentally teach the children misconceptions, unless you are drawing their attention to them so that they do not develop them.

You will need to address misconceptions at various stages in a lesson. These include:

- When children answer questions and demonstrate misconceptions through their answers
- When children are working on a task, and you notice them developing misconceptions
- When you observe children's responses to an assessment for learning task (see Chapters 4 and 6) and notice that they have developed misconceptions

## 3.9 EMBEDDING READING AND WRITING ACROSS THE CURRICULUM

All teachers are teachers of literacy. You should therefore model accurate spelling, grammar and sentence structure when you are modelling writing for children. It is good practice to have subject-specific vocabulary on display in lessons. It is also good practice to use live modelling in writing during lessons that address the foundation subjects as well as in English. This will help to ensure high-quality writing across the curriculum. You should take care to ensure that you use standard spoken English when communicating with children. It is important to plan for opportunities for pupils to develop the skills of reading and writing in all subjects. This enables them to apply the skills that they have developed in English across the curriculum. It is also important to have high expectations of pupils' reading, writing and spoken English in all subjects.

## 3.10 SPACING SUBJECT CONTENT OUT OVER TIME

Research has demonstrated that *the same amount of time spent reviewing or practising leads to much greater long-term retention if it is spread out, with gaps in between to allow forgetting* (Coe et al., 2014, p17). Teachers can address this by revisiting subject content in each of the school terms by checking that prior learning is secure before further developing their knowledge and skills. Moving on to different subject content before revisiting the content allows learners to forget what they have learned. However, revisiting the content in the future enables them to make links with their prior learning and this supports long-term retention.

## 3.11 SCHEMA

Schemas are ways of organising knowledge and storing information in the memory. Over time, schemas change as children accommodate new knowledge. The process of accommodating new knowledge leads to the schema being revised. Children develop a variety of schemas.

## 3.12 INTERLEAVING

Interleaving is the practice of mixing different kinds of problems or tasks within a single lesson. This promotes a high level of cognitive challenge because it stimulates thinking and activates neural connections in the brain. Examples of interleaving are provided later in this chapter.

## 3.13 CONCRETE REPRESENTATIONS IN MATHEMATICS

Providing children with concrete representations is an effective way of supporting their subject-specific understanding. As children learn, they move from concrete representation to abstract thinking. Concrete representations in mathematics include a variety of practical manipulative resources, including counters, blocks and place-value apparatus. Children initially rely on these resources to develop their understanding of specific mathematical concepts and skills. They progress from concrete resources to visual representations. An example is where a child moves from using counters or blocks to support addition to using visual representations – for example, drawings or working out on paper. Eventually, the child can learn in a more abstract way. In this example, the child may start to use a variety of mental methods to solve addition problems.

## 3.14 MOVING FROM CONCRETE REPRESENTATIONS TO ABSTRACT LEARNING

As we have outlined above, children move from using concrete representations to more abstract learning. In geography, it makes sense for them to learn about the geography of their school before they progress to learn about the geography of their local area, the geographical features of the United Kingdom or the wider world. In history, younger children can develop their understanding of chronology by creating their own timeline to show changes that have occurred over their lives. As they progress, they can learn to develop a more abstract understanding of timelines by placing periods of history into chronological sequence. In mathematics, they will gradually develop their mathematical fluency by using a variety of mental methods rather than relying on the use of manipulatives. In science, children need to investigate scientific concepts using materials and models before they can be expected to understand more abstract ideas.

These examples illustrate how children progress from concrete learning to abstract learning. However, it is important that you recognise that children operate at vastly different stages of development. Some children require concrete representations to support their learning well into Key Stage 2 and beyond. It is important not to move children away from using concrete representations too quickly because their subsequent learning may then not make sense.

## 3.15 APPLICATION OF KNOWLEDGE

The skill of applying knowledge and skills is a higher-level skill than simply retaining and understanding knowledge. It is important that you support your pupils to apply their understanding of subject-specific content to different contexts. Examples include:

- Teaching the concept of evaporation in science and then applying that concept to puddles drying up.

- Teaching children a specific technique in art and then asking them to use that technique within a piece of artwork.
- Teaching addition in mathematics and then asking pupils to solve a word problem that requires them to use addition.
- Teaching children the names of shapes in mathematics using plastic shapes and then asking them to locate shapes in the environment.
- Teaching pupils what an adverb is in grammar and then requiring them to use adverbs in a piece of writing.

You will be able to think of other examples of applications. It might not be possible to build applications into every lesson and there is no requirement to do this. Instead, you might choose to focus on teaching pupils subject-specific knowledge and skills, and the application of that subject content might come later during a sequence of lessons. However, in some lessons, it might be possible to move straight from teaching knowledge and skills to developing their skills in applying these.

## 3.16 SYSTEMATIC SYNTHETIC PHONICS

The *Rose Report* (Rose, 2006) recommended synthetic phonics as the best approach for beginning readers and, due to this recommendation, synthetic phonics has been a government policy focus since this time. There is no space here to cover everything you need to know, but the key information is as follows:

- Synthetic phonics breaks a word down into its smallest units of meaningful sound – for example, **b-oa-t** or **c-r-i-s-p.**
- A phoneme is the smallest, meaningful unit of sound within a word – for example, in **b-oa-t**, there are three phonemes but four letters.
- A grapheme is the written representation of the phoneme.
- Blending is the skill of enunciating the phonemes all through the word from left to right to *read* the work – for example, the following three phonemes are enunciated and 'merged' together to read the target word 'shop': **sh-o-p.**
- Segmenting is the skill of hearing the separate phonemes within a word and representing these as corresponding *graphemes* for spelling.
- Children start to learn a simple alphabetic code where each phoneme is represented by a consistent grapheme.

- Once they are secure with the simple code, they progress to a complex alphabetic code. This is where each grapheme can represent different phonemes – for example, **ch**ip, **ch**emist and **ch**ampagne.
- Children use phonics for word recognition and for writing.
- Learning phonics is a time-limited skill that secures accurate word recognition.
- Not all words are phonetically decodable. These are known as exception words – for example, **said.**

## 3.17 ACCOUNTABILITY

You are accountable for children's progress in the national curriculum subjects. The *Education Inspection Framework* (Ofsted, 2019a) includes a renewed emphasis on the wider curriculum, and this has implications for accountability. In subjects such as history, geography, physical education, art, design and technology, and music, it is not enough to know what subject content children have been exposed to. Increasingly, you will be expected to know pupils' starting points in these subjects (what they know and can do), and you will need to be able to identify their next steps in learning. Using assessment in English and mathematics is well embedded in primary schools and teachers are used to being held accountable for children's progress in these subjects. However, assessing children's learning in the wider curriculum is less well established, but is likely to become standard practice over the next few years. It is not enough to communicate to parents in a report that their child enjoyed learning about the Stone Age. In future, you will be increasingly expected to identify what specific knowledge, understanding and skills pupils have secured in history and what they need to learn next.

## 3.18 PREPARING FOR OFSTED 'DEEP DIVES'

The *Education Inspection Framework* (Ofsted, 2019a) includes a new inspection activity which the framework refers to as 'deep dives'. Although you will not be required to participate in this activity as a trainee, it is important to understand what the process involves so that you are prepared for this when you start your teaching career.

The starting point is for you to talk to subject leaders in school about how they prepare for these deep dives. What evidence do they present and what overall narrative are they trying to present to inspectors? Essentially, deep dives allow inspectors to examine specific areas of the primary curriculum in greater depth. They can select any subject so there is significant responsibility on subject leaders to be able to evaluate how well the provision is throughout the school in the area for which they are responsible. Inspectors are particularly interested in looking at curriculum plans to evaluate whether the curriculum is appropriately sequenced across the school. In addition, they are interested in how the subject-specific concepts, knowledge and skills that make subjects unique are taught and sequenced. Inspectors might also be interested in how children are assessed within a subject and how meaningful links are forged between subjects.

The purpose of a deep dive is for inspectors to evaluate the following:

- Curriculum intent – what does the curriculum intend to do?
- Curriculum implementation – how is the curriculum implemented?
- The impact of the curriculum – what progress do children make?

Inspectors might ask subject leaders the following questions:

- *Why is the curriculum structured the way it is?*
- *What are the endpoints of the subject curriculum?*
- *When do pupils start learning the subject curriculum?*
- *What is the approach to assessment in the subject?*
- *How do you ensure that pupils know more, remember more and can do more in the subject?*
- *How do you design the curriculum to address the needs of pupils with SEND or those who are disadvantaged?*
- *How do you ensure the curriculum is ambitious?*

## 3.19 THE WIDER PRIMARY CURRICULUM

The *Education Inspection Framework* (Ofsted, 2019a) requires schools to provide children with a broad curriculum. The primary national curriculum (DfE, 2013) is broad and pupils have an entitlement to study all subjects. Subjects can be combined where there are natural links. However, it is important in your planning that you are familiar with the subject-specific knowledge, concepts and skills that underpin each subject. It is also important that you understand how to sequence these logically to ensure progression in learning. Although cross-curricular approaches do enable children to make meaningful connections between different subjects, it is important that subject-specific knowledge, concepts and skills are taught so that pupils develop secure subject knowledge.

# 3.20 DEVELOPMENTS IN YOUR SUBJECT

You should keep abreast of developments within your subject. Outstanding trainees continue to keep abreast of subject development through:

- Engaging in professional discussions with colleagues
- Observing other teachers
- Joining subject associations – for example, the Geographical Association or Historical Association
- Keeping up to date with the latest research
- Joining online communities of teachers

### TAKE 5

- Good subject knowledge is a key component of effective teaching.
- Good subject knowledge enables pupils to make good progress.
- Subject-specific pedagogy is important: you have to know the subject-specific knowledge, concepts and skills, but you also need to know how to teach these.
- It is important to know the subject-specific knowledge, concepts and skills that make subjects distinct.
- It can be helpful to make meaningful connections between subjects, but the subject-specific knowledge, concepts and skills also need to be taught.

# CLASSROOM EXAMPLE

You need to understand the subject-specific concepts – for example, commutativity – and skills in mathematics. However, it is important that you also understand how children learn mathematics. Effective practice in early mathematics includes the use of manipulative (concrete) resources that support children's understanding of the subject knowledge. These include counters, blocks, place-value apparatus and beads. Both subject knowledge and subject-specific pedagogy are important in supporting children's learning.

Children's understanding of synthetic phonics can be enhanced using practical resources. Magnetic letters and boards help children to physically move letters to build words. Magnetic letters can be moved closer together to develop children's automaticity in blending phonemes for word reading by enunciating each phoneme before identifying the target words. Magnetic letters can also be used to support the process of segmenting words into their constituent graphemes for spelling. Children develop a conceptual understanding of science through working scientifically. They learn scientific knowledge and concepts through scientific investigation. The process of scientific investigation brings science to life because it enables them to experience knowledge and concepts at the same time as developing scientific skills.

## EXAMPLE: LEARNING THROUGH ENQUIRY

- Providing opportunities for pupils to test a range of materials to identify whether they are magnetic or non-magnetic.
- Repeating the activity with a range of metals to demonstrate to pupils that not all metals are attracted to magnets.
- Providing pupils with paper clips and magnets, and asking them how they can work out which magnet is the strongest.
- Using bar magnets to demonstrate the forces of attraction and repulsion.
- Supporting pupils to investigate which materials magnetism travels through and whether this was affected by the thickness of the material.
- Providing a range of materials of different thicknesses to enable pupils to carry out their own investigations.

Children learn history by investigating historical source material. These include primary sources – for example, historical artefacts or diary extracts – and secondary sources – for example, accounts of what life was like in the past written after the time. Through the process of historical investigation, children learn to become historians. They develop their knowledge of historical events and people through investigating a range of source material.

Although enquiry approaches play an important role in learning, it is important that pupils learn the substantive knowledge of the subject through explicit, direct teaching. Pupils should not be left to discover facts through enquiry-based learning because this can result in the development of misconceptions, and it can also result in cognitive load.

## EXAMPLES OF WHAT GOOD SUBJECT KNOWLEDGE LOOKS LIKE IN THE CLASSROOM

Teachers need to understand what progression looks like within specific strands of learning – for example, it is good practice to understand children's development in counting. As children learn to count, they move through a variety of stages before they reach the point of counting using one-to-one correspondence. If teachers understand progression within counting, they can use this to assess which stage children have reached, and they understand how to move their learning forward.

## SUMMARY

This chapter has highlighted how subject knowledge extends beyond the demonstration of knowledge. In doing so, it has emphasised the importance of teachers having a secure understanding of how to communicate effectively subject content to pupils. Effective primary school teachers require a broad body of knowledge to teach across a range of subjects, and this chapter has provided guidance to support you in teaching the curriculum. Specifically, it has outlined the steps that you can take to foster pupils' interest in the subjects that you teach and to ensure that reading and writing are embedded across the curriculum. Strategies to support you in identifying and addressing subject-specific misconceptions have also been offered and some takeaways provided to support your classroom practice.

# 4

# CLASSROOM PRACTICE

## IN THIS CHAPTER

Effective planning and teaching make a significant contribution to pupils' progress over time. As you become more experienced, you will develop your own preferred approaches to planning and teaching, although in all cases it is essential that you adhere to school policies on structuring lessons. There is no correct way to plan and structure lessons, and it is important to acknowledge that it is not necessary to adopt the same approach to planning and structuring for each of the lessons you deliver. However, it is clear that effective planning and teaching rely on the productive use of lesson time, and to support this you may find it helpful to gauge roughly how much time you are devoting to each part of the lesson. Within this chapter, we emphasise the importance of modelling, scaffolding and assessment to support and facilitate pupils' progress and the identification of misconceptions. Questioning is also an integral part of classroom practice, and guidance is offered to support you in using questioning effectively to check pupils' understanding and promote thinking. Additionally, the chapter outlines how metacognitive skills can be developed through planning and teaching, and some practical considerations are identified in relation to the setting of homework.

## KEY RESEARCH

- Spacing out learning: according to Coe et al. (2014), *time spent reviewing or practising leads to much greater long-term retention if it is spread out, with gaps in between to allow forgetting.*
- Interleaving: according to Coe et al. (2014), *learning in a single block can create better immediate performance and higher confidence but interleaving with other tasks or topics leads to better long-term retention and transfer of skills.*

## KEY POLICY

The *Teachers' Standards* state that teachers must:

- *impart knowledge and develop understanding through effective use of lesson time*
- *promote a love of learning and children's intellectual curiosity*
- *set homework and plan other out-of-class activities to consolidate and extend the knowledge and understanding pupils have acquired*
- *reflect systematically on the effectiveness of lessons and approaches to teaching*
- *contribute to the design and provision of an engaging curriculum within the relevant subject area(s)*

(DfE, 2011)

## 4.1 PLANNING SEQUENCES OF LEARNING

Lessons generally fit into a clear sequence, rather than being 'stand-alone'. Teachers need to be able to sequence **components** of knowledge correctly to enable pupils to develop **composite** knowledge. The composite knowledge is the broader learning goal that you intend pupils to achieve after being taught a series of lessons. The goals in the National Curriculum are examples of composite knowledge. They are deliberately broad in scope, and each goal is not intended to be taught in a single lesson. It is useful to think of these goals as the 'bigger picture'. Teachers then need to identify the components of knowledge that pupils need to learn to achieve the broader learning goals. These components of knowledge form the basis of the curriculum that needs to be taught and these become the focus of individual lessons.

The goal is taken from the National Curriculum science document in Key Stage 2:

- Pupils should be taught to construct a simple series electrical circuit, identifying and naming its basic parts, including cells, wires, bulbs, switches and buzzers.

This is an example of composite knowledge. Before pupils can achieve it, they need to learn smaller components of knowledge. Examples of components might include:

- Knowing what an electrical circuit is.
- Knowing what a cell is and its function.
- Knowing the function of wires in a circuit.

- Knowing how to construct a simple circuit to turn a bulb on and off.
- Knowing how to incorporate a switch into a circuit to turn a bulb on or off.
- Knowing how to incorporate a buzzer in a circuit.
- Knowing how to incorporate a switch into a circuit to turn a buzzer on and off.
- Knowing how to incorporate a motor in a circuit (the examples of circuit components need not be limited to the ones identified in the National Curriculum goal).
- Knowing how to make a motor spin in different directions.
- Knowing how to draw a simple circuit.

These components form the basis of the lessons. Teachers will need to sequence the components in a logical way.

## 4.2 PLANNING LESSSONS

At the start of this chapter, it is important to emphasise that there is no correct way to plan and structure a lesson. It is also important to state that it is not necessary to adopt the same lesson structure in each lesson because this can result in children becoming disengaged. However, at the same time, it is important that you follow the school policy on planning and structuring lessons. As you become more experienced, you will develop your own preferred approaches to this.

It is neither the length of a lesson plan nor the time that you spend completing it that is important. It is the thought processes that underpin the planning that are critical to delivering successful lessons. When you plan lessons, you must think very carefully about how to develop pupils' understanding of specific knowledge, concepts or skills. You will need to revisit knowledge, concepts and skills over time to ensure that learning has been retained. When you plan lessons, think carefully about what you want pupils to know, understand or do by the end of the lesson. Break the content down into smaller steps to support pupils to master the intended learning outcome(s). Check their understanding after each step before moving on to the next step.

Schools are taking steps to reduce teacher workload in planning. Therefore, you might be asked to work from planning that teachers have already produced or lesson plans that the school has purchased. Although this is a good way to reduce workload, there is a danger that this approach will mean that you do not develop the skills that you need to be able to plan autonomously. You might go into a school where you are expected to plan autonomously after being in a school where planning was provided for you and in this situation, you might find that you have been deskilled.

# WHAT MATTERS IN PLANNING?

- It is neither the length of a lesson plan or the time that you spend completing it that is important. It is the thought processes that underpin the planning that are critical to delivering successful lessons.
- When you plan lessons, you must think very carefully about how to develop pupils' understanding of specific knowledge, concepts or skills.
- You will need to revisit knowledge, concepts and skills over time to ensure that learning has been retained.
- When you plan lessons, think carefully about what you want pupils to know, understand or do by the end of the lesson.
- Break the content down into smaller steps to support pupils to master the intended learning outcomes.
- Include opportunities to check understanding after each step before moving on.

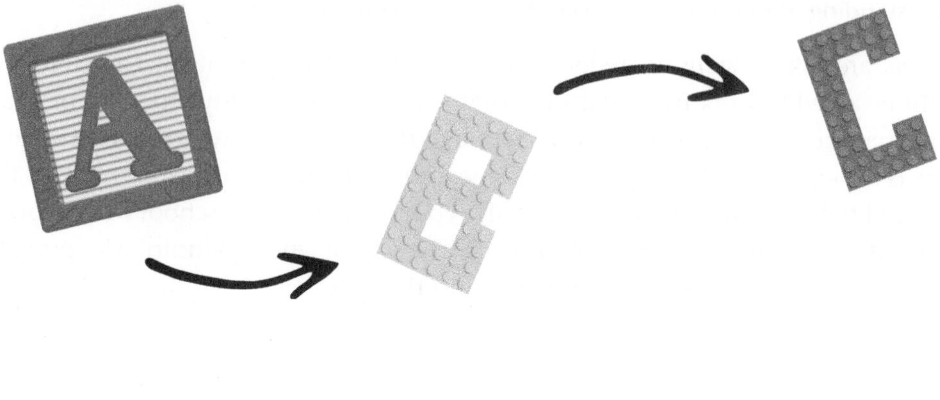

Planning and structuring lessons is a key professional duty of teachers, and it is part of the *Teachers' Standards*. If you are provided with a set of lesson plans, we recommend that, as a minimum, you annotate the plans to identify how they are adapted to meet the needs of your pupils. In addition, you should ensure that the following minimum information is provided on the plan:

- Learning objective(s)
- Early Years Foundation Stage/national curriculum (EYFS/NC) links
- Assessment tasks/opportunities
- Subject-specific vocabulary
- Adaptations for specific pupils or groups

## 4.3 LESSON TIME

It is important to plan so that lesson time is used productively. While there is no need to produce lesson plans that outline the lesson content minute by minute, it is useful to gauge roughly how much time should be devoted to each part of the lesson. Try to allocate sufficient time for pupils to apply their understanding of the lesson content through planning tasks that are motivating and engaging. While you will need to allocate time to teacher exposition (modelling, explaining and questioning), try to reduce the amount of teacher talk in lessons and give children plenty of opportunities to practise their learning in pairs, small groups and individually. When pupils appear to have grasped the content, advance their learning further so that they are cognitively challenged at all stages of the lesson. Extension tasks are useful to provide pupils with additional cognitive challenges.

Consider whether you need all pupils to sit through a lesson introduction or plenary. Would this time be better spent by allocating specific pupils to a task that is precisely matched to their needs, rather than asking them to sit through something they already understand? A more finely tuned approach to teaching will help you target the needs of individuals and groups at different times during the lesson.

## 4.4 MODELLING

It is not enough for you to simply explain to pupils the lesson content – you need to support your explanations with visual modelling. Effective modelling involves several elements, which are outlined below:

- Narrate the thought process: this is addressed below.
- Model the steps through the task: explain the steps, but also represent these visually, perhaps on the whiteboard through diagrams, drawings, models and worked examples. Consider how you will make each of the steps memorable – for example, by using mnemonics.
- Expose the pitfalls they might encounter by highlighting mistakes that are easy to make and explain how to avoid these.
- Combine verbal explanations with graphical representations.
- Use concrete representations to make abstract ideas and concepts more accessible.

You will need to decide how many times you need to model the new content before the pupils begin their task. If they seem unclear, you may need to repeat the modelling several times but vary your approach. Once you have modelled the new learning, build in a formative assessment task to check that your pupils have understood the substantive lesson content. This could include:

- Provide the pupils with a question and then ask them to tell you the steps through the problem.
- Giving them a problem to solve in pairs, which they complete on a small whiteboard.
- Setting them a short, sharp, snappy activity to complete as a group that relates to the lesson content to enable you to check that they have understood.
- Setting them a short quiz.

If the pupils demonstrate misconceptions at this point in the lesson, these will need to be addressed, either with the whole class or specific groups or individuals prior to setting them on tasks. Those pupils who have clearly understood can begin the task immediately.

## 4.5 GUIDED LEARNING: SCAFFOLDING

Guided learning or scaffolding is the process of supporting a learner to develop knowledge, understanding and skills by supporting them through a task. You can scaffold children's learning by initially modelling the subject content or task. Following this, you could then do the task with the pupils. Following the initial modelling of new subject content, one approach to scaffolding is to ask the pupils to work together on an aspect of subject content, either in groups or in pairs. Another scaffolding approach is to ask pupils to explain an aspect of the subject content to the teacher after the teacher has initially explained it to them. You will gradually remove the support as you guide the children towards achieving independence. This is called fading.

# EFFECTIVE MODELLING INVOLVES SEVERAL ELEMENTS:

- Narrating the thought process.
- Model the steps through the task: explain the steps but also represent these visually, perhaps on the whiteboard through diagrams, drawings, models and worked examples. Consider how you will make each of the steps memorable, for example by using mnemonics.
- Expose the pitfalls that they might encounter by highlighting mistakes that are easy to make and explain how to avoid these.
- Combine verbal explanations with graphical representations.
- Use concrete representations to make abstract ideas and concepts more accessible.

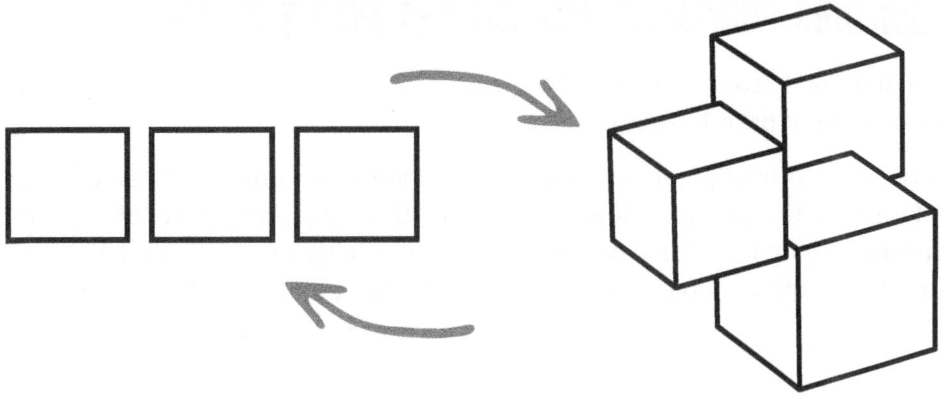

If the pupils are learning something new for the first time, you might need to consider providing them with some resources to support them in completing a task. These resources scaffold the child's learning so that they can complete tasks successfully. Resources that scaffold children's learning can take a variety of forms and might include:

- Writing frames: these are useful if you want the pupils to set out a piece of writing using a structure
- Glossaries with definitions of subject-specific content
- Worked examples or WAGOLLs (What A Good One Looks Like), which are annotated to show the good features
- Steps to success to remind them what they need to do to successfully complete a task
- access to multiplication squares, number lines, counters and vocabulary cards
- access to resources that make abstract ideas concrete – for example, a visual model of a skeleton to show the body's anatomy

Scaffolding can be removed when pupils become more confident so that they do not become dependent on it.

## 4.6 NARRATING THOUGHT PROCESSES

As you model new knowledge, skills or concepts, it is useful to approach this task from the position of a pupil. Try to predict what a pupil might be thinking as they tackle a task. Consider the questions they might ask themselves or what they might think or say as they complete the task. As a teacher, you can then model the new content by 'thinking aloud' so that you narrate the thought processes that you want the pupils to adopt.

## 4.7 BUILDING FORMATIVE ASSESSMENT INTO THE LESSON

At the start of lessons, you should build in opportunities to check the pupils' understanding of prior learning.

You also need to help pupils understand how the lesson content relates to content introduced in the previous lesson. Working through a sequence of lessons is dependent on pupils understanding the prior knowledge and skills they have been taught. This requires more than simply asking the pupils to tell you what they learned in the previous lesson. Planning a formative assessment task at the start of a lesson to check that they have understood the content of the previous lesson is a far more effective way of ensuring that prior learning is secure. Formative assessment tasks should be short, sharp and snappy but provide you with the information that you need to inform your teaching. They might involve:

- A short quiz at the start of a lesson to check pupils' understanding of the previous lesson
- Teacher questioning to ascertain their understanding of previous lesson content
- A quick group activity – for example, matching definitions to terminology on a classroom table: this makes their learning visible
- Providing pupils with an answer and asking them to tell you the question
- Planning a true or false quiz based on previous lesson content

Within a very short time, you should be able to ascertain whether the pupils have developed misconceptions. If they have, these will need to be addressed before you can move on to addressing the new learning. If they seem secure with the content in the previous lesson, you can move on to the new content immediately.

One effective approach is to break tasks down into their constituent components. Providing pupils with clear steps through a task (sometimes referred to as 'steps to success') will help them to remember what they need to do to complete a task successfully. Modelling each of these steps will ensure that pupils understand what they need to do sequentially in order to complete a task successfully.

## 4.8 QUESTIONING

Effective teachers use a range of question types in their teaching to check pupils' understanding and to promote thinking. Effective questioning promotes cognitive challenge and results in pupils developing a more advanced level of understanding of the subject content. Teachers also use questioning to break down problems and to ask pupils to justify their responses. Requiring pupils to respond to questions in full sentences and requiring pupils to use subject-specific technical vocabulary are important teaching skills.

It is important to build in 'wait time' to allow pupils to process the question and to mentally rehearse their response. Sometimes it is useful to ask pupils to think through a question in pairs or small groups so that they are able to scaffold each other's understanding.

## TYPES OF QUESTIONS

- Closed questions: these questions usually have a correct single response.
- Open questions: these questions tend not to have a correct response and might invite several suitable responses. Examples include '**Why do you think**... **think**...**?' or 'What is your opinion on...on...**?' or 'Can you explain why you think this?'.
- Hinge questions: This is where the teacher asks a question and expects a whole class to respond either through a choral response or by asking each pupil to record a response. The pupils' responses enable the teacher to decide what to do next i.e. whether to move on to the next stage in the lesson or whether to re-teach an aspect of subject content.

# 4.9 STRUCTURING LESSONS

Rosenshine (2010, 2012) has developed a set of principles that underpin effective instruction. In summary, the ten principles are as follows:

1. Begin a lesson with a short review of previous learning.
2. Present new material in small steps, with pupil practice after each step.
3. Ask many questions and check the responses of all pupils.
4. Provide models for problem-solving and work examples.
5. Guide pupil practice.
6. Check for pupil understanding.
7. Obtain a high success rate.
8. Provide scaffolds for difficult tasks.
9. Require and monitor independent practice.
10. Engage pupils in the weekly and monthly reviews.

The Dynamic Model (Creemers and Kyriakides, 2006) is an empirically grounded model of teaching, although this is not to suggest that is a correct way to structure a lesson. It includes the elements shown in the table below.

| Aspect of the lesson | Teaching activity |
|---|---|
| **(1) Orientation** | (a) Providing the objectives for which a specific task/lesson/series of lessons take(s) place<br>(b) Challenging pupils to identify the reason why an activity is taking place in the lesson |
| **(2) Structuring** | (a) Beginning with overviews and/or review of objectives<br>(b) Outlining the content to be covered and signalling transitions between lesson parts<br>(c) Drawing attention to and reviewing main ideas |
| **(3) Questioning** | (a) Raising different types of questions - i.e. process and product - at an appropriate difficulty level<br>(b) Giving time for pupils to respond<br>(c) Dealing with pupil responses |
| **(4) Teaching (modelling)** | (a) Encouraging pupils to use problem-solving strategies presented by the teacher or other classmates<br>(b) Inviting pupils to develop strategies<br>(c) Promoting the idea of modelling |
| **(5) Application** | (a) Using seatwork or small-group tasks in order to provide needed practice and application opportunities<br>(b) Using application tasks as starting points for the next step of teaching and learning |
| **(6) The classroom as a learning environment** | (a) Establishing on-task behaviour through the interactions they promote - i.e., teacher-pupil and pupil-pupil interactions<br>(b) Dealing with classroom disorder and competition through establishing and using rules and persuading pupils to respect them |
| **(7) Management of time** | (a) Organising the classroom environment<br>(b) Maximising engagement rates |

*(Continued)*

(Continued)

| Aspect of the lesson | Teaching activity |
|---|---|
| **(8) Assessment** | (a) Using appropriate techniques to collect data on pupil knowledge and skills<br>(b) Analysing data in order to identify pupil needs and report the results to pupils and parents<br>(c) Teachers evaluating their own practices |

*Source:* Cited in Coe et al. (2014, p16).

## 4.10 TEACHER EXPOSITIONS

Explicit, direct teaching is an effective way of ensuring that pupils develop knowledge. When teachers are teaching directly, they might draw on a range of pedagogical approaches to support pupils' learning. These may include:

- Using clear explanations
- Connecting new knowledge to existing knowledge
- Using manipulative resources (counters, blocks and place value apparatus) to explain mathematical concepts or show historical artefacts to develop pupils' historical knowledge
- Using analogies and metaphors to explain complex ideas
- Combining verbal explanations with visual information to support pupils' understanding. This is the use of *dual coding*
- Using demonstrations/ modelling: showing pupils what they need to do rather than just explaining what they should do
- Explicitly focusing on subject-specific vocabulary, ensuring that pupils know and understand word meanings
- Using stories in their teaching to engage pupils and bring the learning experience to life
- Using questioning to check pupils' understanding or to deepen their thinking
- Using mnemonics to help pupils remember things, for example using Big Elephants Can Always Understand Small Elephants to help pupils remember how to spell 'because'
- Explaining common errors/ misconceptions

- Using repetition to reinforce key knowledge
- Explaining the steps through a task
- Using quizzes in teaching to check pupils' understanding
- Summarising key points after information has been conveyed so that pupils know what they need to remember

## 4.11 DUAL CODING

Information is processed in the working memory in specific compartments. Auditory information is processed in the phonological loop and visual and spatial information is processed in the visuospatial sketchpad. Teachers can combine explanations with visual representations, for example by explaining an aspect of subject content and then showing the pupils a diagram or other visual image, which helps them to understand what the teacher has explained. The separate types of information are processed in separate chambers in the working memory and therefore the working memory does not become overloaded. Both the phonological loop and the visuo-spatial sketchpad can work concurrently without reducing the efficiency of the working memory. Cognitive load occurs when one processing chamber becomes overloaded. For example, asking pupils to listen to too many explanations or too many instructions places too great a load on the phonological loop. Many of the studies on visual representations and illustrations (additional images, pictures or icons that symbolise, illustrate or represent content) have reported positive effects, although some studies have reported no effect or harmful effects (EEF, 2021). It is important that images are designed to provide students with information rather than serving decorative purposes to reduce cognitive load. When irrelevant illustrations are added to presentations, this may be a distraction and increase cognitive load rather than supporting the development of schemas (EEF, 2021).

## 4.12 CLASSROOM TALK AND DIALOGIC TEACHING

Paired talk or talk through group collaboration can be an effective tool in the classroom for scaffolding learning, particularly when pupils are placed in mixed-ability pairings or groups.

Dialogic teaching is the process of using talk in teaching to facilitate learning. However, dialogic teaching is an approach that is dependent on interaction between children and teachers, and between children. It is not one-way communication or teacher-directed talk. Through interactive dialogue, teachers can:

- Value children's ideas
- Scaffold children's learning by advancing their current level of understanding
- Use children's ideas to develop richer learning
- Address misconceptions
- Use questions to promote thinking and identify misconceptions

Some teachers avoid this approach to teaching because it might take them away from the script of their lesson plan. However, it is a really effective strategy because it enables you to adapt your teaching to respond to children's needs.

## 4.13 CONSOLIDATION AND PRACTICE

Pupils need time to apply their understanding of lesson content through practice. You need to plan tasks that are sufficiently challenging for all pupils, and you will need to monitor their progress during the lesson to ensure that they are being productive and making progress.

## 4.14 METACOGNITION

Metacognition is the process of *thinking about one's own thinking* (Georghiades, 2004). It facilitates a deeper conceptual understanding of content and more strategic learning. Pupils who have good metacognitive skills can effectively monitor their own learning, regulate their own behaviour, set themselves goals, monitor their own achievement towards these and evaluate their own progress.

Research has found that pupils who employ metacognitive strategies, including self-regulated learning and goal-setting, are more able to engage in cognitive processes, remember information and have a greater capacity for learning (Farrington et al., 2012).

Teachers can model metacognitive strategies by modelling aloud their own thinking, particularly when they explain new subject content to pupils. Metacognitive abilities also can enhance motivation (Cantor et al., 2019) because pupils are aware of their own goals, strengths and weaknesses, and can evaluate their own learning in relation to their goals.

Pupils with good metacognitive skills can:

- Reflect on their strengths and areas of growth
- Self-correct their errors
- Set their own goals

- Take ownership of their own learning
- Engage in regular revision and self-testing
- Act on feedback

(Cantor et al., 2019)

## 4.15 CLASSROOM GROUPING

You will need to make decisions in each lesson on the grouping arrangements that you want to adopt. Consider whether your pupils will be required to work individually, in pairs or in small groups. You will need to identify which pupils work well together and those who do not. Some pupils distract each other and do not work well together. You might wish to consider grouping or pairing pupils of different abilities to provide opportunities for more able pupils to scaffold the learning of those who are working at lower stages of development. Even in classes that are grouped by ability, pupils still operate at varying levels and pupils' level of development can vary from lesson to lesson, depending on what is being taught.

Evidence on the effects of ability grouping suggests that it makes very little significant difference to learning outcomes (Higgins et al., 2014). Research has found that ability grouping can create an exaggerated sense of within-group homogeneity and between-group heterogeneity in the teacher's mind (Stipek et al., 2010).

## 4.16 DEVELOPING A LOVE OF LEARNING

It is important to foster a love of learning. Making learning memorable is one of the joys of teaching. Children have an entitlement to enjoy learning. It is not enough simply to 'push them through' a content-heavy curriculum. Ways of developing a love of learning include:

- Planning an imaginative hook at the start of a lesson to engage the pupils
- Providing opportunities for children to learn through rich, active, first-hand experiences
- Building curriculum experiences around children's interests
- Learning through the outdoors
- Learning through technology
- Learning collaboratively

- Providing a broad curriculum
- Building in educational visits
- Bringing authors, poets, artists and other interesting people into school to work with children
- Allowing children to take risks in their learning

## 4.17 HOMEWORK

The quality of the homework that you provide pupils with is far more significant than the quantity. Homework should provide further opportunities for pupils to consolidate their understanding of the subject-specific content that they have been taught in lessons. It is important not to overload children with homework. The learning that they undertake in the classroom has a far more significant impact than the homework that you set, and homework is ineffective if parents simply complete it for children. As teachers, we must challenge ourselves to ensure that we are setting meaningful homework tasks.

## 4.18 REFLECTING ON LESSONS

A key professional skill is for you to reflect on your lessons. Identify what went well and why. Then consider what needed to be improved and what you might do differently next time. Try to focus your lesson evaluations on children's learning rather than on yourself. So, you should consider what you need to do differently to improve children's learning for individuals and groups. Do not identify too many targets for you to focus on at any one time. It is better to focus on one target and to do it well rather than trying to do too much. Discuss your lessons with your mentors to support the process of reflection. Evaluation does not always have to be written down. It can be done through discussion with others. Ask your pupils what they think you need to get better at. Ask the teaching assistants for their views, too.

### TAKE 5

- Lessons should be carefully structured to ensure that pupils make progress.
- Modelling is a powerful pedagogical tool that enables teachers to demonstrate knowledge, concepts and skills.

*(Continued)*

(Continued)

- Questioning should be used to promote thinking as well as to check pupils' understanding.
- Building assessment into lessons is a key component of effective teaching. It enables teachers to check understanding and address misconceptions.
- Developing metacognitive skills helps children to evaluate their own learning.

## CLASSROOM EXAMPLE

When modelling writing to children, narrating your own thought processes as you write enables children to understand the decisions that authors make when composing a piece of writing. Narrating your thought processes is the equivalent of thinking out loud. Examples of things to say when modelling writing might include the following:

- How shall I start this off?
- Let me think of the sentence I will use and say it out loud first before I write anything.
- I need a better word here. I will use 'shouted' instead of 'said' in this piece of dialogue because it provides more information to the reader.
- I need to use some adjectives here to describe the cave. I will use 'dark' and 'gloomy' because these adjectives help the reader to visualise the cave.
- I want to edit this sentence to make it better.
- I want to include an adverb here to describe how the animal was moving.

Thinking out loud in this way is exactly what you want children to do when they compose their writing. It enables you to model the process of being a writer. As you model the writing, it is important to involve the children in offering suggestions to improve the shared text.

## EXAMPLES OF WHAT GOOD CLASSROOM PRACTICE IN PLANNING AND TEACHING LOOKS LIKE IN THE CLASSROOM

Planning is often more effective when teachers can plan lessons collaboratively. Collaborative planning provides teachers with valuable opportunities to share ideas and resources, and it is a useful form of professional development.

Live modelling in lessons using a visualiser is a very effective way of demonstrating to children the steps they need to work through in their own work. The visualiser can also be used to highlight good examples of work produced by children in the class and for children to assess a piece of work together as a class.

## SUMMARY

This chapter has emphasised the importance of effective planning and teaching, and its contribution to securing pupils' progress over time. It has outlined key research and provided practical guidance on the use of modelling, scaffolding and assessment. We have emphasised that effective questioning can play a crucial role in supporting you in identifying misconceptions and check pupils' understanding. It is essential to remember that the quality of homework is far more significant than the quantity and that children should not be overloaded with homework. It is, therefore, important that teachers challenge themselves to ensure that homework is effective and meaningful. Throughout the chapter, practical examples and takeaways have been provided to illustrate effective practice and to support your professional practice in relation to lesson planning and the delivery of lessons and learning activities.

# 5

# ADAPTIVE TEACHING

> **IN THIS CHAPTER**
>
> It is important that teaching is adapted to address the needs of all pupils and that teachers ensure high expectations and challenges for all children, including those with Special Educational Needs and Disabilities (SEND). The Equality Act (2010) places legal duties on schools and local authorities to protect pupils from direct and indirect discrimination because of their sex, race, disability, religion or belief, or sexual orientation. Similarly, the *Special Educational Needs and Disability Code of Practice* (DfE/DoH, 2015) details the responsibilities of schools in relation to legislation and statutory guidance. Throughout this chapter practical guidance is provided to support schools and teachers to meet the needs of pupils with special educational needs and/or disabilities, and to ensure compliance with legislation and statutory guidance. A range of strategies are highlighted to support your professional practice, and examples and takeaways are provided to illustrate effective practice in relation to the adaptation of teaching.

## KEY RESEARCH

Research by Hart et al. (2004) has demonstrated that grouping pupils by attainment can have negative effects, including reducing teachers' expectations, undermining pupils' dignity and sense of hope, and accessing a restricted curriculum for pupils in low-attainment groups. Furthermore, Slavin's research (1987, 1990) has demonstrated that ability groups do not increase average pupil achievement, but that they do impact detrimentally on the achievement of pupils in lower ability groups. Advocates of ability grouping have emphasised the associated benefits of differentiated teaching and the importance of tailoring the curriculum and pedagogy to the needs of individual pupils (Tomlinson, 2000). However, existing research has highlighted the problems associated with grouping and teaching pupils on the basis of achievement data, particularly for pupils in lower attainment groups (Francis et al., 2017).

Existing research has demonstrated that ability grouping can result in:

- Misallocation of pupils to groups and a lack of fluidity in groups
- Poor quality teaching for pupils in lower groups
- Differential pedagogy which can result in a widening of the achievement gap
- Reduced teacher expectations
- Negative pupil perceptions about themselves

(Francis et al., 2017)

However, despite these concerns, it is also important to consider that research has also demonstrated a range of positive effects in relation to ability grouping (Francis et al., 2017). Steenbergen-Hu et al. (2016) have argued that ability grouping can support schools to individualise instruction. Ireson (1999) has argued that ability grouping provides opportunities for learners to work directly with others whose ability and achievement is similar.

As such, it remains difficult to provide recommendations in relation to grouping arrangements, as the findings of existing research remain inconclusive. However, it is helpful to reflect on existing arrangements and to consider whether mixed-ability grouping may be a suitable alternative to ability grouping within your context. Perhaps most importantly, research by Taylor et al. (2016) suggests that setting by mixed-ability grouping may be a fairer approach. This is because mixed-ability grouping benefits the most and does not punish others to the extent that ability grouping does (Taylor et al., 2016).

## KEY POLICY

The *Teachers' Standards* state that teachers must:

- *know when and how to differentiate appropriately, using approaches which enable pupils to be taught effectively.*
- *have a secure understanding of how a range of factors can inhibit pupils' ability to learn, and how best to overcome these.*
- *demonstrate an awareness of the physical, social and intellectual development of children, and know how to adapt teaching to support pupils' education at different stages of development.*
- *have a clear understanding of the needs of all pupils, including those with special educational needs; those of high ability; those with English as an additional language;*

*those with disabilities; and be able to use and evaluate distinctive teaching approaches to engage and support them.*

(DfE, 2011)

## 5.1 EQUALITY ACT 2010

The Equality Act 2010 identifies disability as a protected characteristic. This places the following legal duties on schools and local authorities:

- They must not directly or indirectly discriminate against, harass or victimise disabled children and young people.
- They must make reasonable adjustments to prevent disadvantage.
- They must have regard to the need to eliminate discrimination, promote equality of opportunity and foster good relations between disabled and non-disabled children and young people.

Discrimination might be evident if children with SEND are denied admission to a school because of their needs. It is also evident when children with disabilities are subjected to bullying. In addition, if schools fail to ensure that children with SEND have equality of opportunity by allowing them to be educationally disadvantaged, this might also constitute discrimination. Schools should, therefore, provide reasonable adjustments to ensure that children with SEND have the same educational opportunities as other children. However, what constitutes a reasonable adjustment is inadequately defined. What might be reasonable to one person may not be considered by another person to be reasonable. This places schools in a vulnerable situation, particularly if parents feel that reasonable adjustments have not been made.

The requirement of schools to foster good relationships between disabled and non-disabled children is often inadequately addressed in schools. Although schools often make great efforts to meet the needs of children with SEND, fostering good relations is not just about preventing bullying. It requires schools to consider how fostering good attitudes towards people with disabilities can be embedded through:

- Curriculum subjects, so that children begin to understand that people with disabilities can be high achievers
- The physical environment, including displays that positively affirm disability
- Resources that positively affirm disability
- Disabled staff working in the school

This is not an exhaustive list. However, schools play a critical role in changing people's attitudes towards individuals with minority identities. Children need to know that prejudice and negative stereotypes are harmful. They need to recognise that disability is not a negative attribute. This will support social inclusion within society by fostering the development of positive attitudes towards difference and promoting the importance of demonstrating respect towards others, regardless of people's differences.

## 5.2 CODE OF PRACTICE

The *Special Educational Needs and Disability Code of Practice* (DfE/DoH, 2015) is a statutory framework that schools must follow to meet the needs of pupils with special educational needs and/or disabilities. It is a lengthy document that includes guidance for schools and local authorities. Irrespective of whether schools have opted out of local authority control, the local authority has a legal obligation to ensure that the needs of these pupils are met.

According to the code:

> *A child or young person has SEN if they have a learning difficulty or disability which calls for special educational provision to be made for him or her.*
>
> (DfE/DoH, 2015, p15)

In addition:

> *A child of compulsory school age or a young person has a learning difficulty or disability if he or she: has a significantly greater difficulty in learning than the majority of others of the same age, or has a disability which prevents or hinders him or her from making use of facilities of a kind generally provided for others of the same age in mainstream schools or mainstream post-16 institutions.*
>
> (DfE/DoH, 2015, pp15–16)

The *Code of Practice* emphasises the importance of working in partnership with children and parents. Pedagogical approaches for supporting children with SEND are often recommended by experts. However, it is also important to seek the views of children and their parents. Children and parents should be involved in all decisions that are made in relation to school-based provision. They should be involved in identifying goals and in reviewing the progress that has been made towards these. Schools are legally required to consider how the views of all children can be sought, including those with impaired or no verbal communication skills. This is inadequately addressed in the *Code of Practice*.

It is also important to remember that some parents of children with special educational needs may also have their own complex needs. Some parents may be reluctant to work in partnership with schools for various reasons, and it is important for school leaders and teachers to work to establish positive and trusting relationships with all parents.

Once children have been identified as having a special educational need and/or disability, they move on to a stage that is referred to in the *Code of Practice* as SEN Support. This does not necessarily result in securing additional funding and support for the child but allows the school to adopt a 'graduated approach'. The graduated approach involves four phases that support the school to meet the needs of the child. These include:

- Assess: Determining the child's current level of achievement
- Plan: Planning to meet the needs of the child through adaptive teaching and targeted interventions
- Do: Implementing adaptive teaching and interventions
- Review: Evaluating the success of the strategies that have been implemented in partnership with children and parents

The aim of the graduated approach is designed to ensure that children's needs are identified early and addressed. It supports schools in narrowing gaps between children with and without disabilities.

Some children with more complex needs may require a statutory assessment by the local authority to determine whether the child needs an Education and Health Care Plan (EHCP). The purpose of an EHCP is to make special educational provision to meet the specific needs of the child or young person, to secure the best possible outcomes for them across education, health and social care, and, as they get older, prepare them for adulthood.

## 5.3 WHAT IS ADAPTIVE TEACHING?

Adaptive teaching is not the same as differentiation. Traditional approaches to differentiation typically involve grouping learners by ability and allocating work with varying levels of challenge to match learners' needs in those ability groups. This practice serves to widen achievement gaps between different groups of learners.

Adaptive teaching is the practice of ensuring that all pupils can achieve their full educational potential. It requires teachers to consider how they might adapt a particular task, or their teaching more generally, to ensure that pupils with SEND and those with English as an Additional Language (EAL) are not disadvantaged from achieving the outcomes that they can achieve. Sometimes, this will mean that all pupils can work on the same subject content, but some pupils may need specific adaptations to enable them to learn the same content that their peers are learning. It requires teachers to consider how they might break down subject content further for specific pupils, what additional resources and support specific pupils might require enabling them to learn the subject content and what additional teaching specific pupils may need to enable them to keep up with their peers.

## 5.4 A WORD OF CAUTION

Pupils do not have different styles of learning. Learning style theory which categorises pupils into specific learner types has been discredited and it is not helpful to assume that pupils with SEND and those with EAL learn differently from their peers. Some pupils may need repeated exposure to specific components of knowledge. They may need subject interventions to enable them to catch up and keep up with their peers. They may need specific aspects of knowledge broken down further so that knowledge is introduced in bite-sized chunks (chunking). They may be working on developing automaticity with a component of essential foundational knowledge which they need to learn before they can progress further through the subject curriculum. However, most pupils with SEND and those with EAL do not learn in a different way from their peers. All pupils can benefit from practices such as dual coding where visual content is introduced alongside written or auditory content. All pupils can benefit from the use of manipulative resources to support their understanding of subject-specific content. Most pupils can benefit from pre-teaching from time to time. All pupils need access to high-quality teaching which is characterised by a culture of ambition and high expectations. There may be some exceptions, for example pupils with highly complex needs, including those with profound and multiple learning disabilities (PMLD). These pupils may need access to a sensory curriculum, but it is extremely unlikely that they will be placed within a mainstream education setting.

## 5.5 HIGH EXPECTATIONS

Where children with SEND can learn the same curriculum as their peers, they are better off doing so. This may not always be the case and some pupils with highly complex needs may need a tailored curriculum which addresses their individual needs. The National Curriculum is intended for all pupils. Most pupils with SEND should be working towards achieving the same National Curriculum goals as their peers. They should be following the same curriculum trajectory, although they may be working at an earlier stage of development. This is because teachers should prioritise ensuring that the pivotal foundational knowledge is secure before moving pupils too quickly through the curriculum. Some pupils with SEND may need repeated exposure to specific components of knowledge, resulting in them needing to master earlier concepts to automaticity.

Children with SEND can thrive and achieve well if teachers have high expectations of them. It is important to raise your expectations so that children with SEND have equality of opportunity. Many learners with SEND can demonstrate very high levels of achievement, particularly if their needs do not relate to learning and cognition difficulties. Even in cases where children do have learning and cognition needs, they can achieve highly if the teaching is adapted to meet their needs and if teachers have high expectations of them. SEND is not synonymous with low achievement.

One of the key challenges for schools is low teacher expectations. Too often, children with SEND are placed in 'low-ability' groups. They are provided with work that is less challenging and consequently, they do not achieve as well as their peers who do not have SEND. Sometimes, they are provided with tasks that address lower-level learning outcomes, and tasks are elaborately differentiated and often dumbed down.

Children with SEND do not always require different tasks. They can often achieve the same learning outcomes as other children if they are given additional support to help them do so. Sometimes, a task can be adapted to enable children to achieve the same learning outcomes by breaking it down into smaller steps or by providing additional resources or time to complete the task. Children with SEND do not automatically require specialist teaching. High-quality inclusive teaching is beneficial to all learners, not just those with SEND.

There may be occasions when children with SEND need to work on different learning outcomes and different tasks. However, this should not be the default strategy. Where possible, you should aim to adapt your teaching so that all children achieve the same learning outcomes. This will support you in narrowing the achievement gaps.

## 5.6 ADAPTIVE TEACHING STRATEGY: PRE-TEACHING

Many children with SEND and those with EAL will benefit from pre-teaching, which provides an opportunity for you to teach the knowledge, concepts and skills that you will cover subsequently in the lesson. This ensures that they are not placed at a disadvantage during the lesson because they might take longer to process the subject content. Pre-teaching can be used to develop familiarity with key texts, vocabulary, concepts, knowledge and skills prior to the lesson so that they can participate more effectively during the lesson.

## 5.7 ADAPTING LESSONS TO MEET THE NEEDS OF ALL LEARNERS

Adapting your lessons to meet the needs of all learners ensures that you are meeting your duty of providing reasonable adjustments in line with the Equality Act 2010. Depending on the subject content, there are various ways of adapting your lessons described next.

## 5.8 ADAPTING LESSONS: SOME PRACTICAL SUGGESTIONS

- Provide additional adult support to specific children
- Provide additional resources for specific children, including manipulatives, number lines, hundred squares, vocabulary mats and writing frames
- Provide some learners with additional time to complete tasks
- Break down a task further into very small steps to enable children to meet the learning outcomes
- Provide individual support to children when teachers are directly teaching subject content to ensure that pupils have understood it
- Provide opportunities for pupils to consolidate their learning by repeated practice
- Provide sentence stems to support children with writing sentences
- Provide multisensory approaches so that learners can learn through their senses
- Provide additional adult support to enable children with SEND or EAL to complete tasks
- Provide additional resources for specific children, including manipulatives, number lines, hundred squares, vocabulary mats, and writing frames
- Provide some learners with additional time to complete tasks
- Break down a task further into very small steps to enable children to meet the learning outcomes
- Provide individual support to children when teachers are directly teaching subject content to ensure that pupils have understood it
- Provide opportunities for pupils to consolidate their learning by repeated practice
- Provide multisensory approaches so that learners can learn through their senses

## 5.9 OVERLEARNING, CONSOLIDATION AND PRACTICE

Many children benefit from opportunities to consolidate their knowledge, understanding and skills before moving on to the next stage of learning. Some pupils require repeated exposure to specific aspects of subject content in order to learn that content to automaticity. This is often referred to as overlearning. This does not just apply to children with SEND. When you plan sequences of lessons, consider building in opportunities to revisit subject content which has already been taught. Always build in retrieval tasks to support the retrieval of prior knowledge at the start of lessons and throughout lesson sequences. Before moving on to something new, provide children with opportunities to apply their understanding of subject content in different contexts to ensure that they are developing higher-level thinking and independence skills. For example, pupils may know how to complete a calculation but applying the same calculations skills to a mathematical word problem deepens their understanding. Planning frequent opportunities during lessons for pupils to work on subject content will support pupils to develop automaticity with that subject content. It is important for teaching assistants to encourage children to complete tasks independently rather than fostering a culture of dependency. It is also important for teaching assistants to have high expectations of all children.

## 5.10 REFRAMING QUESTIONS

During your lessons, you will plan to use questioning to develop pupils' understanding of the subject content and to check their understanding. Through reframing questions, you can ensure that children with SEND can participate fully in the lesson. Different strategies for reframing questions include:

- Breaking down a larger question into a series of smaller questions which then lead to the larger question
- Using manipulatives as you ask the question to support children in processing the question
- Using real-life contexts within a question to make the question more relevant
- Modelling the child's response to a question by writing what the child says on the board
- Asking a closed question
- Allowing children with limited or no verbal communication to respond to questions by selecting from choices using pictures, signs or technology

## 5.11 EFFECTIVE DEPLOYMENT OF TEACHING ASSISTANTS

Teaching assistants need to be deployed to support pupils' learning at every stage of the lesson. During the introduction to a lesson, you might ask them to work with specific children who might benefit from subject content being re-explained or further broken down. Try to keep all children in the lesson where possible rather than send children out of the lesson to work with a teaching assistant.

During the main part of the lesson, it is important that children with SEND receive as much support from the teacher as other children do. The teaching assistant should not always work with children with SEND because they will benefit from being taught by a teacher. It is important that teaching assistants focus on helping pupils to learn rather than focusing on supporting children to complete tasks. This involves them using high-quality questioning to extend children's thinking skills.

Schools deploy teaching assistants to improve outcomes for students with SEND. However, research demonstrates the following:

- The ineffective deployment of teaching assistants does not lead to improved student outcomes.
- Students with the highest levels of SEND often make the least progress due to ineffective deployment arrangements.
- When they are well-trained and used in structured settings with high-quality support and training, teaching assistants can make a noticeable positive impact on student learning.

(Sharples et al., 2015)

## 5.12 FLEXIBLE GROUPING ARRANGEMENTS

Children with SEND will benefit from a flexible arrangement for grouping. Sometimes, you may decide that their needs are best targeted in ability groups, although it is important to remember that they will be working at different stages of development in different strands of learning. A flexible approach to ability grouping enables you to move children to different ability groups, depending on the subject content that is being taught. In addition, children with SEND should also have opportunities to work in mixed-ability groups so that they are exposed to higher-level thinking and more advanced language and communication.

## 5.13 COMMUNICATION AND INTERACTION NEEDS

Children with communication and interaction needs constitute a broad group. This category of needs includes children with speech, language and communication requirements, including those with autistic spectrum conditions. These children often need time to process their responses and they often respond well to praise. It is important not to finish their sentences off for them or to hurry them up when they are speaking. Children with limited or no verbal language skills can be supported to communicate using pictures, signs and symbols. Some children may benefit from a tightly structured communication programme through which they learn to develop the skills of social communication. Some children may also benefit from a highly structured programme through which they learn to develop their vocabulary.

Children with autism can benefit from the use of visual timetables, social stories, and a social and emotional regulation intervention programme to address broader aspects of their needs.

## 5.14 COGNITION AND LEARNING NEEDS

Children with cognition and learning needs include those with moderate learning difficulties (MLD), specific learning difficulties (SpLD), including dyslexia, and PMLD. This is a broad group with wide-ranging needs. The approaches outlined earlier in this chapter will support children with MLD. Children with SpLD such as dyslexia may benefit from highly structured phonics, reading and writing interventions. Children with PMLD will benefit from a highly personalised sensory curriculum. Children who fall into this category are usually taught in specialist provisions.

## 5.15 SOCIAL, EMOTIONAL AND MENTAL HEALTH NEEDS (SEMH)

Again, this is a broad group. Children with Social, Emotional and Mental Health Needs (SEMH) may include those who demonstrate challenging behaviour, those who struggle with emotional regulation and those with specific mental health needs, including anxiety, depression, self-harm, those with eating disorders or those who have experienced grief and loss.

To address the needs of those with challenging behaviour, you need to implement the school behaviour policy. However, it is also important to remember that all behaviour is a form of communication and often it is a way of demonstrating an unmet need. Children may demonstrate inappropriate behaviour due to lack of boundaries at home, experiences of adverse circumstances and poor attachment with their primary carer. They may have low self-esteem. It is important to implement strategies in partnership with children and parents, and to set small but achievable goals. The needs of children with poor mental health are best addressed through a whole-school approach to mental health.

## 5.16 SENSORY AND PHYSICAL NEEDS

Children with sensory or physical needs include those with visual or hearing impairment and those with physical disabilities. Again, this constitutes a broad group of learners. Many of these pupils do not have learning and cognition problems, and may be operating at a high stage of cognition. It is important to ensure that the work you set for them is challenging and that you provide appropriate adaptations to support them in their learning. Examples may include the use of enlarged text, clear instructions, supported by visual cues, adapted equipment and hearing loops.

## 5.17 PUPILS WITH ENGLISH AS AN ADDITIONAL LANGUAGE (EAL)

Children with EAL do not necessarily have special educational needs. Their difficulties in learning may arise because they are in the process of learning another language rather than due to an underlying difficulty. They will benefit from being immersed in a social and communication-rich environment. They may benefit from a structured language and communication intervention. Using pre-teaching vocabulary and texts is a useful strategy to maximise their participation during lessons. Aim to support your explanations and modelling with visual cues, manipulatives and other resources. Provide concrete manipulative resources to support their learning and allow them to code-switch between English and their first language if they cannot identify the word in English.

## 5.18 MEETING THE NEEDS OF HIGH-ACHIEVING PUPILS

Some children in your class will require tasks that require additional cognitive demands. They may be 'outriders' in that they may be working at a level above anyone else in the class in specific subjects. It does not follow that they will demonstrate this same level of achievement across all subjects. These pupils still need to feel part of a group and part of a classroom. They should not be separated from others to work individually because this fosters a sense of exclusion. You might need to provide them with a different task, but it is good practice to still have them seated at a table with other pupils. Strategies for challenging these pupils include:

- Having specific questions in your lesson which you directly ask these children to respond to
- Setting a task that focuses on the same content as the rest of the class, but that promotes a higher level of thinking – for example, some children need to focus on the application of knowledge to extend their learning, while others may focus on understanding knowledge which is a lower level of thinking
- Setting an open-ended problem-solving task which has multiple solutions
- Expecting greater productivity and quality of work – for example, in writing tasks
- Developing mastery in a specific learning objective by applying the learning to different contexts
- Working on a learning objective from a higher level year group, provided that prior learning has been mastered

**CHILDREN WITH ENGLISH AS AN ADDITIONAL LANGUAGE DO NOT NECESSARILY HAVE SPECIAL EDUCATIONAL NEEDS.**

Their difficulties in learning may arise because they are in the process of learning another language rather than due to an underlying difficulty.

### TAKE 5

- High-quality teaching for all children raises outcomes for children with SEND.
- Differentiated activities may be necessary some of the time, but they should not be the automatic response because setting different tasks can widen ability gaps.
- Children with SEND should receive the same amount of time from a teacher as other children.
- Teaching assistants must be deployed effectively so that they do not create a dependency culture and they should aim to promote learning rather than prioritising task completion.

## CLASSROOM EXAMPLE

Pre-teaching is particularly useful in English to familiarise children with a specific text. Children can develop familiarity with the book. The session can also be used to identify specific vocabulary that is included in the text that children may not know. The session can therefore be used to teach children this vocabulary.

## EXAMPLES OF WHAT GOOD PRACTICE IN ADAPTIVE TEACHING LOOKS LIKE IN THE CLASSROOM

Children with dyslexia have difficulties with reading and writing. The process of writing is rarely automatic for these children. It is often a very slow, laborious process. It requires them to synthesise a range of skills and knowledge, including letter formation, spelling, sentence structure and grammatical knowledge. One way of adapting your teaching is to ask the pupils to produce an annotated drawing, poster or presentation slides to reduce the emphasis on writing. They might benefit from using a computer to word process their work. In addition, you could provide software that converts speech to reduce overload.

## SUMMARY

This chapter has focused on strategies to support you in addressing children's diverse needs. It has emphasised the need to ensure high expectations and challenge for all children, including those with SEND. It has also outlined the implications of legislation and statutory guidance, and it is essential that you are aware of your roles and responsibilities in relation to these. Additionally, it has highlighted a range of common special educational needs, and it has identified strategies for addressing these, including for those who have EAL. Finally, it is essential to acknowledge that children's needs can be diverse and multiple and that in many cases they do not fit into a single category that can be addressed using a single strategy. As such, teaching must be both proactive and reactive to the individual and specific needs of all pupils.

# 6

# ASSESSMENT

## IN THIS CHAPTER

This chapter outlines the importance of formative and summative assessment in the primary classroom. Effective formative assessment enables teachers to identify children's current stages of development so that they can identify their next steps in learning. It is a process that enables planning and teaching to be responsive to the needs of individuals and groups of learners. It is essential that formative assessment is not a bolt-on to effective teaching, but instead, it is seen as integral to it. It supports teachers to check on children's learning within lessons and it enables them to identify and address misconceptions. As such, it is a key professional skill. Similarly, the chapter argues that well-designed summative assessments can also be used by teachers to identify gaps in pupils' learning. Conducting a question-level analysis of pupils' answers to test questions is one example of the ways in which summative assessment data can be used to identify specific patterns. Despite this, the purpose of summative assessment is primarily to support the processes of school evaluation and inspection. This chapter explores the difference between formative and summative assessment and the importance of each in supporting approaches to teaching and learning.

## KEY RESEARCH

According to seminal research from Black and Wiliam:

> *There is a body of firm evidence that formative assessment is an essential component of classroom work and that its development can raise standards of achievement. We know of no other way of raising standards for which such a strong prima facie case can be made.*
>
> (Black and Wiliam, 1998, p12)

> It is **ESSENTIAL** that formative assessment is not a bolt-on to effective teaching.
>
> Formative assessment must be seen as integral to effective teaching.
>
> Formative assessment supports teachers to check on children's learning within lessons and it enables them to identify and address misconceptions.
>
> It is a **KEY PROFESSIONAL SKILL**.

Black and Wiliam (1998) emphasised the following:

- Feedback should focus on the quality of the work and include advice on how to improve it. It must avoid comparisons with other pupils.
- Formative assessment is particularly beneficial for low-achieving pupils.
- Pupils' self-assessment is an important and effective method of formative assessment, but only if pupils understand the overall intentions of the task.
- Providing time for pupils to respond to questions by thinking them through with their peers is essential.

- Frequent short tests during a unit of work can provide useful feedback both to pupils and teachers rather than fewer long tests. However, providing marks or grades rather than feedback is counterproductive as pupils will focus on these rather than the feedback.
- Effective teaching cannot be separated from formative assessment. Effective teachers use assessment during their teaching rather than teaching and assessing learning at a later point.
- A classroom culture that promotes questioning and deep thinking in which pupils learn from shared discussions with peers and teachers is essential to effective teaching.

## KEY POLICY

The *Teachers' Standards* state that teachers must:

- *know and understand how to assess the relevant subject and curriculum areas, including statutory assessment requirements.*
- *make use of formative and summative assessments to secure pupils' progress.*
- *use relevant data to monitor progress, set targets, and plan subsequent lessons.*
- *give pupils regular feedback, both orally and through accurate marking, and encourage pupils to respond to the feedback.*

(DfE, 2011)

## 6.1 FORMATIVE ASSESSMENT

Formative assessment has traditionally been referred to as *Assessment for Learning* (AfL), although it is important to note that the ITT Core Content Framework (CCF) adopts the phrase *formative assessment* and does not use *AfL*. One definition is offered below:

> *Assessment for Learning is the process of seeking and interpreting evidence for use by learners and their teachers to decide where the learners are in their learning, where they need to go and how best to get there.*
>
> (Assessment Reform Group, 2002)

Formative assessment is usually informal. Teachers use it during lessons and between lessons to identify what learners know and can do, and to determine misconceptions. Formative assessment supports teachers to:

- identify what learners know and can do.
- identify and address misconceptions or gaps in pupils' understanding.
- plan for/identify pupils' next steps in learning.
- adapt their teaching during lessons to support pupils' understanding.
- evaluate the effectiveness of their own teaching.
- identify pupils who need specific interventions.

Formative assessment supports children to:

- understand what they know and can do.
- know what they need to do next.
- know how to get there.

Formative assessment is designed to support the learner. The processes that underpin formative assessment rarely involve assigning marks or grades to pupils. Formative assessment helps teachers identify pupils' current stages of development, their misconceptions and the next steps in learning. It supports pupils to understand what they have achieved and to know their next steps in learning. It is, therefore, a form of assessment that should be done *with* children rather than *on* children.

Formative assessment takes a variety of forms, and these are outlined in the remainder of this chapter. It is important to remember that all assessments should be supportive and positive rather than negative. When assessment is used effectively, it protects and increases children's self-esteem. In contrast, when formative assessment is ineffective, it damages children's self-esteem. You should therefore consider carefully the impact that verbal and written feedback can have on children's self-worth.

## 6.2 WHAT IS THE PURPOSE OF ASSESSMENT?

Assessment should enable teachers to know whether pupils are making progress. Effective assessment helps teachers to identify what pupils know, understand and can do and to plan for their next steps in learning. When assessment is formative then it informs teaching. Through assessment, teachers can identify and address misconceptions in learning to enable pupils to make greater progress.

## 6.3 WHAT DO WE MEAN BY PROGRESS?

If the purpose of assessment is to enable teachers to know if pupils are making progress, it is important that teachers understand what is meant by progress. Progress is no longer measured through scores on a test. Simply, pupils make progress when they know more, remember more and can do more in a subject. The subject curriculum should be designed to ensure that pupils know more, remember more and can do more. Therefore, pupils simply make progress when they are learning the curriculum.

## 6.4 SO HOW DO I MEASURE PROGRESS?

If schools are no longer evaluating pupils' progress based on scores, then how is progress captured? One of the best ways of evaluating whether pupils are making progress (i.e. learning the curriculum as intended) is to talk to pupils about their learning. From these conversations, it will be quite easy to establish if pupils know and remember the essential components of knowledge that have been identified in the subject curriculum. Can they identify and explain subject-specific concepts? Can they remember what they learned last week or last term? Looking through a sample of pupils' books will help you to gauge what pupils know and can do and lesson visits will enable leaders to judge whether the subject curriculum is being learned as intended.

## 6.5 AVOIDING MISLEADING FACTORS

When teachers are in the process of assessing what pupils know, remember and can do, it is important not to be over-influenced by misleading factors. One example of a misleading factor is how busy pupils are in a lesson. Pupils may be busy and on task, but this does not mean that they have learned the intended curriculum. Pupils may be diligently getting on with their work, but it is only through talking to them and looking at their work that you will be able to ascertain if pupils have learned the intended curriculum. Positive attitudes to learning should be celebrated but are not necessarily a benchmark of what pupils know, understand and can do. Equally, negative learning behaviours are undesirable but are not necessarily an indicator that pupils have not learned the intended curriculum.

**PROGRESS = KNOW MORE, REMEMBER MORE, DO MORE IN SUBJECTS**

**LEARNING THE INTENDED CURRICULUM = PROGRESS**

## 6.6 SUMMATIVE ASSESSMENT

In contrast, a summative assessment is a summary of a child's achievement over time. It is usually formal and takes the form of tests and examinations. However, judgements of pupils' learning can be based on teacher assessments of pupils' performance over time – for example, by considering their performance across a series of tasks.

Unlike formative assessment, summative assessment is primarily used to help schools to evaluate their effectiveness. It often takes the form of grades, and this enables stakeholders to hold the school to account. It enables school leaders to demonstrate to pupils, parents, governors, local authorities, the Department for Education and Ofsted how the school is performing. Summative assessments are also used to evaluate overall teacher performance.

Well-designed summative assessments can be used by teachers to identify gaps in pupils' learning. One example of this is the process of conducting a question-level analysis of pupils' answers to test questions. This analysis enables teachers to identify specific patterns – for example, if many pupils struggle with a specific question on a test, the teacher can subsequently revisit this in their lessons. Although summative assessment grades can help pupils gain a sense of their overall achievements, the purpose of summative assessment is primarily to support the processes of school evaluation and inspection.

## 6.7 CHECKING PRIOR KNOWLEDGE: RETRIEVAL PRACTICE

At the start of a lesson, it is important to establish pupils' prior knowledge. It is not enough to simply ask pupils to tell you what they learned in the previous lesson. You need to check that prior knowledge is secure before you move on to something new. When planning sequences of lessons, it is important to structure knowledge, concepts and skills sequentially so that children make progress in their learning. If prior knowledge is insecure, it will need to be revisited before you can effectively move pupils on to the next stage in their learning.

One useful way of assessing prior learning is to ask the pupils questions at the start of the lesson to check their understanding of the subject content in the previous lesson using a retrieval task. You will need to consider how to maximise pupils' participation so that you are not relying on a small number of pupils to give you the answers. One way of maximising participation is to ask the children to write the answer to a question on a small whiteboard. You can then ask them to show you the answer.

Another strategy for checking on prior learning is to make use of technology. Voting pads are ideal for multiple-choice questions as they allow pupils to select an answer from a choice. The answers of all pupils are then displayed on the screen, which enables you to identify if there are any general misconceptions in pupils' understanding. These can then be addressed immediately.

You can set the pupils a task to complete in pairs or in small groups at the start of a lesson. For example, if you want to check pupils' understanding of odd and even numbers, you could ask them to work as a group at a table and sort numbers into these two categories. Set them a specific time for this task and use a timer so that they can see how long they have left to complete the task. This also fosters a sense of urgency. When they have completed this task, you will then easily be able to ascertain if they have any misconceptions.

Building in short and snappy formative assessment tasks at the start of lessons will enable you to see if knowledge and skills have been retained from the previous lesson. Quizzes, questioning, paired tasks and group tasks are relatively straightforward to design. If many children demonstrate misconceptions at this point in the lesson, you may have to adapt the lesson on the spot to address these. If individual pupils, rather than many pupils, demonstrate misconceptions, these can be addressed specifically with those individuals during the lesson.

## 6.8 QUESTIONING

Effective questioning enables you to promote children's understanding further during lessons. It also enables you to check pupils' understanding and identify misconceptions and gaps in understanding. It is, therefore, a pedagogical approach that supports both teaching and assessment. Question types can include closed questions where there is often a very specific answer or open questions that require pupils to explain, justify, compare, synthesise and evaluate. Open questions therefore promote higher-level thinking. Higher-order questions usually start with words such as 'how', 'what' or 'why'. These questions place additional cognitive demand on pupils because they require pupils to think about something rather than just recollect something.

It is crucial to plan questions related to the intended learning outcomes of the lesson. Although some of your questioning during lessons will inevitably be unplanned and responsive to pupils' needs, planned questioning can ensure that pupils develop higher-order thinking skills.

Plan to use open and closed questions throughout the lesson. Closed questions generally require pupils to recall some information and open questions increase cognitive demand by developing higher-order thinking skills.

Consider how you will maximise pupil participation when you ask questions. A hands-up approach is rarely effective because it allows some children to dominate the lesson and at the same time it allows some children to opt out of participation. After you have asked a question, provide them with an opportunity to process the question and to think through their response before expecting an answer. Building in adequate wait time ensures that all children have an opportunity to process a response and it therefore supports inclusion.

Research has found that the questions used by teachers are often insufficiently challenging for the students (Flórez and Sammons, 2013). In addition, studies have found that the time given to elaborate on an answer is often too short (Condie et al., 2005; Gipps et al., 2005; Kellard et al., 2008; Kirton et al., 2007; Webb and Jones, 2009). Research has recommended increasing the time given for students to think of an answer (Webb and Jones, 2009) and making greater use of open questions rather than closed questions (MacPhail and Halbert, 2010) to promote higher-order thinking. Creating a positive classroom climate in which misconceptions are addressed enables students to learn from mistakes (Torrance and Pryor, 2001) and promotes learning. Specific questions should be planned to check students' understanding or to promote thinking. Questions that require students to give more detailed or multiple responses than a single correct answer are more effective at promoting thinking (MacPhail and Halbert, 2010).

## 6.9 STRUCTURING LEARNING

One effective strategy for structuring lessons is to break down the subject content into a series of sequential steps or stages during the lesson. After each step, provide the pupils with an opportunity for guided practice by setting a short task. This can take various forms, including setting individual, paired or small group tasks and subsequently providing pupils with feedback. Alternatively, you might choose to work through a task with the whole class after you have modelled the subject content by asking the children to tell you how to complete the task. At each step, plan the questions that you will ask the pupils to either check on their understanding or promote higher-level thinking.

# EFFECTIVE QUESTIONING . . .

- Enables you to promote children's understanding further during lessons.

- Allows you to check on pupils' understanding and identify misconceptions and gaps in understanding.

- Supports both teaching and assessment.

- Question types can include . . .
  - Closed questions which require pupils to **explain**, **justify**, **compare**, **synthesise** and **evaluate**.
  - Open questions which start with words such as ***'how'***, ***'what'*** or ***'why'***.

These questions place additional cognitive demand on pupils because they require pupils to think about something rather than just to recollect something.

## 6.10 ADDRESSING MISCONCEPTIONS

It is important that you create a positive environment in your classroom so that children are not afraid to make mistakes. Children's misconceptions provide you with feedback which informs your teaching. If they are not addressed, there is a risk that children will not develop an accurate understanding of the subject content. Carefully designed questions can help you to identify misconceptions. In addition, you need to carefully monitor children's understanding during the time that they work on a task. If you notice that children have developed misconceptions, then you can provide them with individual support to help them overcome these. This may include additional modelling, scaffolding or use of questions to develop their understanding.

If you notice that several pupils have developed a common misconception during a lesson, one strategy is to draw these children together and reteach the subject content. If many children have developed misconceptions in relation to specific subject content, this should prompt you to reflect on your own teaching. You might need to reteach the subject content to the class in a different way.

Regardless of organisational matters, it is important to unpick children's misconceptions. Through effective use of questioning, you should try to ascertain how the misconception has developed. It is important not to simply tell children that they are 'wrong', but to explain to them what their misconception is.

Misconceptions can also be identified through marking children's work. Once these are identified at this stage, you can then plan to address them in the next lesson. One useful strategy is to highlight to children what the common misconceptions are in relation to subject content when you introduce new subject content. Highlighting misconceptions to pupils in this way minimises the chance that they will make the same errors because you have already alerted them to these.

## 6.11 SELF-ASSESSMENT

Self-assessment is a valuable skill for children to develop. Through this process they learn to appraise their own work by identifying their achievements and areas for improvement. Self-assessment is also a life skill. As adults, being able to make judgements about our own performance at work helps us to identify our strengths and also the actions we need to take to improve further. It drives self-improvement.

To be effective, children need to know and understand what criteria they are using to assess their work. You should establish clear success criteria for the task so that pupils understand the elements that should be present throughout the work. Children can then look for these and identify whether they have achieved the success criteria.

However, to drive improvement, it is more effective for children to view self-assessment as a continuous process rather than simply a process which they complete when a piece of work has been finished. By continually referring to the success criteria during task time, they can identify whether there are elements that still need to be included to complete the task successfully.

## 6.12 PEER-ASSESSMENT

Peer-assessment enables children to provide each other with feedback on their work. However, as with self-assessment, children need to be provided with clear success criteria so that they know how to evaluate the work of their peers. In addition, children might need support in how to write peer feedback so that their feedback is both positive but also developmental. They may need to be introduced to some key underpinning principles of peer-assessment. These include:

- Always give more praise than criticism.
- Always provide your peer with a target which relates to the success criteria.
- Use the success criteria to assess the work rather than making general comments.
- Treat the work of your peer as confidential.

You will need to create a positive culture in the classroom so that children know that it is acceptable to make mistakes and that mistakes are an essential part of the learning process.

## 6.13 REDUCING WORKLOAD IN MARKING

You should mark children's work regularly and follow the school's marking policy. Some schools have begun 'sampling' children's books rather than marking every child's book after a lesson to reduce teacher workload. Many schools now use live feedback in lessons. This is where teachers circulate the room and provide pupils with feedback. Another approach is to show pupils correct responses (e.g., sharing good examples) to questions and ask them to mark their own work. Whole class marking also ensures that pupils receive rapid feedback, and it reduces the burden for teachers. Marking a **sample** of books allows you to identify generally what children have understood. It also enables you to identify common misconceptions. You can then address these in the next lesson.

Marking can be time-consuming, but the use of codes to represent feedback can speed up the process. Again, you should follow the policy in your school. One effective strategy is to live mark a piece of work in class using the visualiser. This enables children to understand what a good piece of work looks like and how work is evaluated by the teacher.

## 6.14 FEEDBACK

Research from Hattie and Timperley (2007) suggests that models of feedback should address three questions:

- Where am I going?
- How am I going?
- Where to next?

According to Hattie and Timperley (2007), the answers to these questions enhance learning when there is a discrepancy between what is understood and what is aimed to be understood. It can increase effort, motivation or engagement to reduce this discrepancy, and/or it can increase cue searching and task processes that lead to understanding (thus reducing this discrepancy). Feedback is among the most critical influences on pupil learning. A major aim of the educative process is to assist in identifying these gaps ('How am I going?' relative to 'Where am I going?') and to provide remediation in the form of alternative or other steps ('Where to next?').

Feedback comments should be specific rather than general. Comments such as 'good work' are unhelpful because this does not communicate to pupils why the work is good. More specific praise is beneficial – for example, 'This character description is good because you have used some good adjectives'.

Identify what the child has done well in relation to the success criteria and provide them with a target. Ensure that you provide them with time to address this target during the next lesson. Not all written feedback has to demonstrate this level of detail. Some schools now only provide detailed feedback on specific pieces of work rather than on every piece of work. It is not appropriate to overload children with too much feedback and with too many targets. One or two carefully considered targets within each unit of work is probably enough to advance their learning. It is also not appropriate to write extremely detailed comments on their work because many children will simply not read them.

Try to make greater use of verbal feedback during lessons. This is instant and helps children to make greater progress immediately. It is also more meaningful to children because it can be supported with non-verbal cues which also provide children with feedback on their work.

## 6.15 SHOWING MODELS OF GOOD WORK

Sharing models of good work or WAGOLLs (What a Good One Looks Like) when you are modelling a task helps children to understand what they need to do to be successful. It is important to analyse the work with the children by explaining why it is a good piece of work. It is sometimes useful to share weaker examples of work with children, but you must explain to children why these are not good examples. WAGOLLs can be displayed on working walls and shared with children on the board or screen, or by using a visualiser.

## 6.16 TEACHER ASSESSMENT OVER TIME

The process of analysing children's knowledge and skills over time and making a judgement that best represents what they have achieved is referred to as teacher assessment. Selecting the best pieces of work that represents what children can achieve over time is a fairer way of formulating a judgement than asking them to complete a test in timed conditions. Teacher assessment judgements can be formulated from a range of evidence, including:

- Samples of children's work
- Your observations of children
- Children's performance in low-stake tests – for example, weekly tests or end-of-unit tests
- Photographs that capture the process of learning
- Discussions with children about their learning

## 6.17 INVOLVING CHILDREN IN FORMATIVE ASSESSMENT

One of the key principles of formative assessment is that children should be partners within the process. At the start of this chapter, we highlighted the importance of doing assessment *with* children rather than *on* children. Traditionally, children's perspectives on their learning have not been sought.

Involving children in formative assessment includes seeking their perspectives on their learning – what they have achieved so far and what they need to do to improve further. Discussions can be scheduled at fixed points during the year to ascertain children's perspectives. You can support children in this process by providing them with samples of their work. You can then look at this work together and support the child to identify strengths and targets for development.

### TAKE 5

- Formative assessment improves achievement.
- It enables teachers to check understanding and address misconceptions, and it informs planning.
- Summative assessment provides a summary of a child's achievements at a specific point in time.
- Plan to use formative assessment during lessons.
- Plan your questions on your lesson plan.

## CLASSROOM EXAMPLE

Questioning plays a crucial role in supporting teachers to find out what pupils already know and to identify gaps in knowledge and understanding. This enables teachers to effectively scaffold in order to close the gap between what is known and what still needs to be learned. There is a range of approaches to questioning that can be used, and it is important to understand the variety of question types that can be used. Open-ended questions allow pupils to develop their responses and demonstrate understanding of a specific concept or topic. Hinge questions can also be used to check that pupils understand at a 'hinge-point' within the lesson. This is the point at which you move from the teaching of one idea, topic or concept to the teaching of another. The purpose of a hinge question is to ensure that pupils understand the prerequisite content that has been taught before the next chunk of learning is delivered. This enables the teacher to identify whether it is appropriate to move on, which is crucial when pupils are required to understand one concept in order to access another.

Examples of hinge questions include:

- Where is the verb in this sentence?
- Which of the following demonstrates an example of alliteration?
- Which of these is not a trapezium?
- What is the difference between a verb and an adverb?

## EXAMPLES OF WHAT GOOD PRACTICE IN ASSESSMENT LOOKS LIKE IN THE CLASSROOM

Effective questioning and assessment should provide opportunities for pupils to access and demonstrate higher levels of understanding. When planning these opportunities, it is helpful to consider Bloom's (1956) taxonomy, which positioned thinking skills within a hierarchy from the lowest level to the highest level of thinking. These are shown below:

- Knowledge (lowest level)
- Comprehension
- Application
- Analysis
- Synthesis
- Evaluation (highest level)

When planning questioning and assessment activities, it is important to reflect on the decisions that you have made in order to ensure that pupils are able to demonstrate the full breadth and depth of knowledge and understanding that they have acquired and developed.

## SUMMARY

Effective formative assessment enables planning and teaching to be responsive to the needs of individuals and groups of learners. It is essential that it is not a bolt-on to teaching and learning. Instead, it is integral as it supports teachers to check on children's learning within lessons in order to identify and address misconceptions. Summative assessment also plays a crucial role in teaching and learning as it informs teachers' professional practice and encourages reflection. Throughout this chapter, takeaways and examples have been provided to support your approach to assessment, and relevant research has been outlined to underpin this discussion.

# 7

# MANAGING BEHAVIOUR

## IN THIS CHAPTER

It is important to teach children to demonstrate positive learning behaviours. This chapter outlines strategies to support you in managing children's behaviour in the primary classroom. Children in primary schools learn best when they develop warm, trusting and consistent relationships with their teachers and other adults. They also need clear, consistent routines and clear boundaries so that they understand what is expected of them. This chapter identifies some key strategies that will support you in managing pupil behaviour.

## KEY RESEARCH

Through operant conditioning, a child makes an association between a behaviour and a consequence (Skinner, 1938). The underlying principle is that positive reinforcement of good behaviour strengthens that behaviour. Positive reinforcement is best explained as the addition of a stimulus (reward) to increase the likelihood of a positive behaviour being repeated. Learners are rewarded for good behaviour and good work so that they will continue to demonstrate positive behaviour and produce high-quality work due to the likelihood of receiving the reward again. In classrooms, rewards may take the form of stickers, stamps, certificates or simply verbal praise. The problem with positive reinforcement is that it promotes extrinsic rather than intrinsic motivation. Learners demonstrate extrinsic motivation when they are only motivated to complete a task because of the reward that they will receive when the task has been completed. Intrinsic motivation is demonstrated when learners are motivated to complete a task because they enjoy the task, are engaged by it and are immersed in their learning. Most teachers want learners to be intrinsically motivated rather than extrinsically motivated. There is also a danger that 'empty' praise (praise when it is not really deserved) can foster a culture of low expectations (Coe et al., 2014).

In contrast, negative reinforcement (often incorrectly associated with punishment) is the removal of a negative stimulus to enable individuals to achieve their goals. The removal of a negative stimulus strengthens the likelihood of achieving the target goals. An example of negative reinforcement is outlined as follows. A child with autistic spectrum conditions is completing a task in a mainstream classroom, which provides them with sensory overload. The child finds it difficult to learn because the classroom is too noisy, and the child is distracted by the colourful displays. The child decides to go and work in a quiet study space. This is a space in the classroom that is separated by a partition so that the child can focus on their work without distraction. The child can complete the task successfully by removing the adverse stimulus (noise and colour).

Punishment can be positive or negative. Positive punishment is the addition of something that reduces the likelihood of the behaviour occurring again. Examples might include:

- The introduction of a report card system to monitor learners' behaviour in each lesson
- A phone call home to parents to report poor behaviour

Negative punishment is the removal of something to decrease the likelihood of behaviour occurring again. Examples include:

- The loss of break time
- The loss of privileges
- The loss of free time – for example, detention
- Moving a child away from their friends in class.

The problem with behaviourist approaches is that they do not address the causes of behaviour – they only address consequences. Learners' behaviour is often rooted in social circumstances and their behaviour is often an attempt to communicate an unmet need. In contrast, humanist approaches assume that teachers need to pay attention to the needs of the whole child rather than simply focusing on consequences. Humanists such as Carl Rogers and Abraham Maslow are often viewed as the founding fathers of humanism. Rogers emphasised the need to build learners' self-esteem and the need for unconditional positive regard. Maslow, in his hierarchy of needs (Maslow, 1943), demonstrated that children cannot achieve their full potential unless their basic physiological needs, safety needs and their need to feel loved are addressed first.

The **PROBLEM** with behaviourist approaches is that *they do not address the causes of behaviour*. They only address consequences.

Learners' behaviour is often rooted in social circumstances and their behaviour is often an attempt to communicate an unmet need.

**HUMANIST** approaches assume that teachers *need to pay attention to the needs of the whole child* rather than simply focusing on consequences.

## KEY POLICY

The *Teachers' Standards* state that teachers must:

- *have clear rules and routines for behaviour in classrooms, and take responsibility for promoting good and courteous behaviour both in classrooms and around the school, in accordance with the school's behaviour policy.*
- *have high expectations of behaviour, and establish a framework for discipline with a range of strategies, using praise, sanctions and rewards consistently and fairly.*
- *manage classes effectively, using approaches which are appropriate to pupils' needs in order to involve and motivate them.*

- *maintain good relationships with pupils, exercise appropriate authority, and act decisively when necessary.*

(DfE, 2011)

## 7.1 ESTABLISHING EXPECTATIONS

Mentors will check your expectations of learners' behaviour in lessons. Establishing high expectations for behaviour will minimise disruption and maximise time for learning for everyone. You will need to work hard with classes initially to ensure that you consistently reinforce your expectations. High expectations may include:

- Insisting that they work in silence at specific times when you ask them to work independently
- Ensuring that they are looking at you and listening to you when you are speaking to them – 'books closed, pens down, look this way'
- Insisting that they persevere with tasks that they find difficult
- Establishing clear rules about movement around the room and sticking to a seating plan
- Setting clear expectations about participation in group work
- Being clear about how much work you expect them to complete in a specific time
- Managing transitions effectively as learners move from one activity to the next
- Establishing a reasonable working noise level
- Ensuring that learners attend lessons punctually
- Ensuring that learners bring the correct equipment with them to lessons

## 7.2 DEVELOPING POSITIVE ATTITUDES TO LEARNING

Inspectors will look closely at attitudes to learning in lessons. They will look at whether learners are interested, motivated and engaged in their learning. They will evaluate the extent to which they listen carefully, persevere, ask questions, challenge each other respectfully, take ownership of their learning and work independently. These positive characteristics may need to be taught and consistently reinforced during lessons.

## 7.3 DEVELOPING POSITIVE RELATIONSHIPS

Establishing positive relationships with learners is the starting point to support you in developing good behaviour management. While this will not necessarily guarantee good behaviour, it will reduce the likelihood of negative behaviour occurring. Learners generally do not learn from teachers they do not like. Your learners need to know that:

- you care for them as people as well as caring for their learning.
- you understand them.
- you believe in them.
- you will forgive them when they get things wrong.

Although you will need to establish clear behavioural expectations in every lesson, learners generally enjoy lessons if they like the teacher. Try not to shout unless necessary and deal with issues firmly but calmly. It is easier to start firmly and then subsequently relax with a class. All learners will test you at first, so a 'no-nonsense' approach is best adopted. You should find that when learners are clear about your behavioural expectations, you will then be able to relax with them and demonstrate a sense of humour as time progresses. Simple and effective ways of establishing relationships with new classes include the following:

- Learn the names of all learners very quickly; a seating plan will help with this
- Smile
- Try to get to know your learners, including their interests outside of school
- Thank them for their contributions in class
- Acknowledge the effort they make with their work
- Create a 'can-do' culture so that learners start to believe in their abilities
- Apologise to learners if you make a mistake
- Tell them a little about yourself
- Be enthusiastic about your teaching; if you are excited it will be infectious
- Use eye contact
- Use their names in class

# YOUR LEARNERS NEED TO KNOW THAT:

- you care for them as people as well as caring for their learning;
- you understand them;
- you believe in them;
- you will forgive them when they get things wrong.

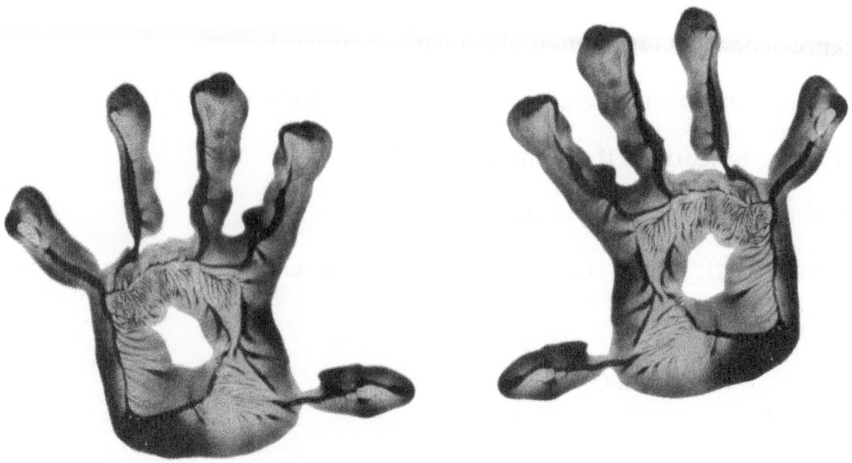

## 7.4 A PREDICTABLE AND SECURE ENVIRONMENT

Pupils need to feel safe in school. Some pupils do not live in safe environments at home and for some, their communities may not provide a sense of safety. It is critically important, therefore, that all pupils feel that they are safe in school. The school leadership team will seek to establish a culture which supports all pupils and staff to feel safe. One aspect of keeping all children safe is for all schools to have robust policies for addressing bullying and safeguarding more broadly. If pupils feel secure and safe in their environment, they are more likely to thrive.

Most pupils like a sense of routine. This fosters a sense of security. It is important to remember that some pupils may become distressed if there are sudden and unexplained changes to their daily routines, for example, autistic children. In busy schools, changes to daily routines are inevitable but it is important to try to warn children in advance so that the change of routine does not come as a shock. Keeping a consistent subject timetable, having a clear routine for the beginning and end of days, and maintaining clear routines at the beginning and end of lessons all support pupils to feel secure.

## 7.5 RULES AND ROUTINES

Establishing clear expectations for learners' behaviour is critical, and it is important that you follow the whole school policy in relation to rules and routines. Simple strategies such as greeting the learners as they enter the classroom set the correct tone for the rest of the lesson. Displaying a task on the board for them to do as soon as they sit down ensures that there is no wasted learning time, and this will minimise disruption. Establish clear expectations about punctuality to lessons and implement sanctions if learners turn up late to lessons. Read the school behaviour policy and ensure that you are familiar with the rules and routines of the school. If these are consistently applied by all teachers, learners clearly understand what is expected of them. Establish basic expectations. These include the following:

- When you talk, they must listen.
- Insist that they listen carefully when other learners are answering questions or making other contributions to the lessons.
- Insist that they value everyone's contribution.
- Establish a zero-tolerance policy on the use of bad language in class and implement sanctions where necessary.

- Develop clear rules on whether movement around the classroom is permitted.
- Develop clear routines and expectations at the end of lessons – for example, tidying away, pushing chairs under desks, picking things up from the floor – and explain clearly what they should do if you are still talking and the bell goes.
- Develop rules for classroom talk – when it is allowed and when it is not.
- Develop clear rules for tasks – be clear about whether they should be working individually or whether they are allowed to collaborate.
- Ensure that they do not eat food in lessons or chew gum.
- Not permitting the wearing of hats or coats in the classroom.
- Not permitting disrespect of school property – for example, by adding graffiti onto their exercise books.

These are examples of classroom rules, but your school behaviour policy will guide you on the expectations. If you notice low-level disruption, nip this in the bud immediately by challenging it. Ignoring it creates a culture of low expectations and often the problem will escalate if it is unchallenged.

## 7.6 PRAISE AND REWARDS

Take every opportunity to praise good behaviour and good effort in class, and by sending e-mails and text messages to parents. Assign rewards in line with the school policy. Although learners generally enjoy receiving praise and rewards, and their use results in other learners modifying their behaviour, there are some issues that you need to be aware of, such as:

- The overuse of praise can result in a culture of low expectations, particularly when praise is given when it is not really deserved.
- The overuse of praise can result in learners working hard only because they want a reward; this promotes extrinsic motivation rather than intrinsic motivation.
- Rewards and praise tend to be assigned to learners who do not demonstrate consistently good behaviour; when they suddenly modify their behaviour, they tend to receive praise or rewards.
- Some learners never receive rewards or praise; these tend to be learners who work hard and behave well consistently.

## 7.7 USING SANCTIONS

Sanctions should be applied either when learners' attitudes to learning are not good or when they demonstrate inappropriate behaviour, and they should generally be a last resort. You must implement sanctions in line with school policy during your lessons and they should be proportionate to the incident that warranted their use.

## 7.8 CLASSROOM MANAGEMENT

One effective strategy for developing good classroom management is to implement a seating plan. This enables you to know learners' names quickly and to separate learners who are likely to disrupt each other. Follow the school policies on whether learners are allowed to leave their seats during lessons and the school policy on toilet use during lessons. Make sure that your expectations are clear from the moment they enter the room. Giving them a task to do immediately is one way of settling them down and focusing them on learning.

## 7.9 BUILDING SELF-ESTEEM

Self-esteem can influence pupils' behaviour. Pupils with overall low self-esteem may display emotional regulation difficulties which need to be supported. Overall self-esteem is made up of **self-concept** and **self-efficacy**. Self-concept is a person's view of themselves, and this is influenced by a range of external influences, including parents, peers, teachers and other influences in the child's ecological system. Self-efficacy relates to how competent individuals are at completing tasks. In cases where self-efficacy and self-worth are both low, overall self-esteem will be low. In cases where self-worth and self-efficacy are both high, overall self-esteem will be high. However, some individuals may have low self-worth, but high self-efficacy and others may have high self-worth and low self-efficacy. In these cases, and in cases where self-worth and self-efficacy are both low, pupils may demonstrate defensive behaviours and they also struggle to regulate their emotions. Improving self-esteem through improving achievement is a powerful way of boosting overall self-esteem and improving behaviour.

## 7.10 MOTIVATION

Motivation can influence behaviour. If motivation is **extrinsic**, pupils are likely to be motivated by rewards and this will drive task completion. Learners who demonstrate **intrinsic** motivation are motivated purely by the task itself rather than rewards and praise. Teachers should foster intrinsic rather than extrinsic motivation by explicitly modelling their own motivation and teaching pupils that they can gain enjoyment from completing a learning challenge without gaining a reward for doing so.

Research demonstrates that improving achievement enhances motivation and confidence. It has been argued that:

> *Teachers who are confronted with the poor motivation and confidence of low attaining students may interpret this as the cause of their low attainment and assume that it is both necessary and possible to address their motivation before attempting to teach them new material. In fact, the evidence shows that attempts to enhance motivation in this way are unlikely to achieve that end. Even if they do, the impact on subsequent learning is close to zero . . . the poor motivation of low attainers is a logical response to repeated failure. Start getting them to succeed and their motivation and confidence should increase.*
>
> (Coe et al., 2014, p23)

## 7.11 BUILDING RESILIENCE

Resilience can be understood in different ways. Learners are resilient when they can 'bounce back' from a negative experience (e.g., if they score low in a test). Resilience can also be demonstrated by persevering with a task, even when the task is challenging. Resilient learners tend not to give up! Resilient learners also know to seek help when they need it. From these descriptions, it is clear to see how low resilience can negatively influence behaviour. Learners who are not resilient may not persevere with tasks, they may not seek help when they find something difficult, and they may find it difficult to recover from 'failure'. Teaching children about the importance of being resilient as a key component of the curriculum can therefore be beneficial.

## 7.12 PROMOTING POSITIVE LEARNING BEHAVIOUR

In recent years, there has been a move away from the term 'behaviour management' to 'behaviour for learning', despite the former term being adopted in the *Teachers' Standards*. Learners demonstrate good learning behaviour when they are:

- Listening
- Collaborating
- Asking questions
- Challenging other people's opinions about subject content

- Persevering when they find something difficult
- Managing distractions
- Making connections between different aspects of learning
- Noticing
- Being independent
- Using tools for learning when they become 'stuck' rather than depending on a teacher

Some learners find it difficult to participate in lessons. They do not ask questions and they tend to be passive. Quiet, passive and compliant behaviour is not good learning behaviour. You need to encourage your learners to ask questions, to affirm other people's responses or to challenge them, and to keep trying when they are working on a really difficult problem. Effective learners manage their distractions well. If there is disruption taking place, or if someone walks into the room to talk to you, effective learners manage these distractions well and continue with their tasks. Some learners waste valuable learning time when they become 'stuck' in their learning. This stops them from making progress in the lesson. By teaching the learners a four-step process, you can offer them a framework to guide their response when this happens. When learners become 'stuck', you can encourage them to:

- **T**hink
- **T**alk to a peer
- Use **T**ools for learning (resources to help them with their learning)
- **T**alk to a teacher

The four Ts approach ensures that the last thing they will do if they become stuck is to ask a teacher. When you see learners demonstrating good learning behaviours you should provide positive descriptive praise – for example, 'I liked the way you persevered with that task, Sam'; 'I saw some really great collaboration in that group'.

## TAKE 5

- Children's behaviour is shaped by a variety of factors.
- It is often an attempt to communicate an unmet need.

*(Continued)*

(Continued)

- All children benefit from clear, consistent routines.
- Praise is always more effective than sanctions.
- Strategies that are effective with one child may not be effective with another.

## CLASSROOM EXAMPLE

- Remember that behaviour management is a proactive as well as a reactive approach to the management of behaviour. You should support pupils by teaching them what is expected and how this will help them to be successful.
- Assert your own norms to reduce the likelihood of pupils looking to one another for cues about what is and is not acceptable.
- Take time and effort to develop routines and ensure that you teach these explicitly and reinforce them consistently over time.
- Use consistent consequences to remind pupils that they have not met the classroom norms, rules and routines.
- Do not hesitate to use sanctions when it is necessary to do so in response to norms and rules being broken. Ensure that all sanctions are applied consistently and with certainty.
- Use a combination of intrinsic and extrinsic rewards to encourage positive behaviours.

## EXAMPLES OF WHAT GOOD PRACTICE IN BEHAVIOUR LOOKS LIKE IN THE CLASSROOM

A solution-focused approach enables you to set achievable goals with children with specific and challenging behaviour needs – for example, pupils in alternative provision. A solution-focused approach enables you to set achievable goals with children with specific behavioural needs. The strategy uses a variety of techniques. These include:

- Scaling: 'On a scale of 1–10, where would you rate your behaviour?' 'Why have you made that choice?' 'Let's set a goal to get a little better'. 'Where would you like to be on this scale next term?' 'What will you be doing differently then?'

- Complimenting: 'What are you good at?' 'What would your friends/parents say that you are good at?'
- Exception-finding: 'Tell me about a time when you had the same problem [for example, being angry] but the problem didn't last as long'. 'Tell me about a time when you have been the best version of yourself'.

Solution-focused strategies are positive strategies that enable children to understand they can sometimes make the correct choices. They seek to improve children's self-esteem, confidence and motivation.

## SUMMARY

This chapter has outlined your roles and responsibilities in relation to teaching children how to demonstrate positive learning behaviours. It has discussed strategies to support you to manage children's behaviour and it has provided examples and takeaways to illuminate effective practice and support your professional reflection. Key research has been highlighted to underpin the arguments that have been put forward and we have emphasised the importance of pupils developing warm, trusting and consistent relationships with teachers and other adults.

# 8

# PROFESSIONAL BEHAVIOURS

## IN THIS CHAPTER

It is essential that teachers uphold the highest standards in relation to personal and professional conduct. Teachers must also uphold public trust and maintain professional boundaries with pupils and their parents. Additionally, trainees will work closely with mentors and colleagues, including teaching assistants (TAs), and effort should be invested in establishing effective and professional relationships with all members of staff. As a trainee, you will need to take some responsibility for your own professional development and you will need to learn from and respond to feedback, reflect on progress, and engage with research and literature to underpin your practice. This chapter provides practical guidance to support you in building effective relationships and taking responsibility for your own professional development. It also offers support to enable you to address any challenges you experience in relation to workload time and well-being. Finally, it explains your responsibilities in relation to safeguarding and it emphasises your role in contributing to the wider life of the school.

## KEY RESEARCH

In 2015, the Education Endowment Foundation (EEF) published its report on the use of TAs. The report was provided in order to offer practical and evidence-based guidance to help primary and secondary schools make the best use of TAs. Within the report, there are seven key recommendations:

- TAs should not be used as an informal teaching resource for low-attaining pupils.
- Use TAs to add value to what teachers do, not replace them.
- Use TAs to help pupils develop independent learning skills and manage their own learning.
- Ensure TAs are fully prepared for their role in the classroom.

- Use TAs to deliver high-quality one-to-one and small-group support using structured interventions.
- Adopt evidence-based interventions to support TAs in their small-group and one-to-one instruction.
- Ensure explicit connections are made between learning from everyday classroom teaching structured interventions.

## KEY POLICY

In 2019, the Department for Education published its *School Workload Reduction Toolkit* (DfE, 2019b). This provides practical resources for school leaders and teachers to help reduce workload, and it was produced by school leaders and teachers in conjunction with the Department for Education (DfE). The toolkit has been tested with a range of schools in England and the resources should be used to:

- identify workload issues in your school.
- address workload issues in your school.
- evaluate the impact of workload reduction measures.

## 8.1 WORKING WITH MENTORS

Your mentor plays a crucial role in your development as a teacher. Effective mentors provide you with support, expert guidance through coaching and mentoring, and a suitable level of challenge to enable you to improve your effectiveness as a teacher. In addition, your mentor will play a major role in assessing your development against the *curriculum* that your Initial Teacher Education (ITE) provider has developed in partnership with its schools. Therefore, it is important that you invest effort into establishing effective, professional relationships with your mentor.

Although your mentor also plays a role in developing effective relationships with you, there are things that you can do to quickly gain their support and trust. These include:

- Being willing to learn from their expertise
- Acting on their advice and feedback
- Asking for help when you need it
- Meeting deadlines

- Being organised for lessons
- Completing planning and marking in a timely fashion

Most mentors will go out of their way to support a trainee teacher who is trying exceptionally hard to be the best teacher that they can be. However, mentors can quickly become irritated when trainee teachers fail to act on their advice and unprofessional behaviour is rarely tolerated in schools. This includes poor attendance and punctuality without good reasons. It is your responsibility to establish effective, professional relationships with your mentors so you must prioritise this.

Although you are part of the teaching profession, it is important to remember that during your initial training, you are not a qualified teacher. Inevitably, things will happen in school that will annoy and upset you. Knowing when to voice your opinion and when not to is part of learning to tread a very fine professional line as a trainee teacher. In some cases, it might be more appropriate to talk to your Initial Teacher Training (ITT) managers, tutors or lecturers about your concerns and take their advice about whether it is appropriate or otherwise to voice your opinions in school.

Mentors love it when trainees demonstrate initiative. They often enjoy working with trainees who have great ideas, and they tend to like it when trainees excite and motivate them. This is often a reason for agreeing to host a trainee. One of the most exciting aspects of mentoring a trainee is the opportunity it creates to learn from someone who has been exposed to the latest pedagogical ideas and research. Some mentors are very open to learning from their trainees and others are less so. You will quickly ascertain the type of mentor you have been allocated. Some mentors will give you free rein in the classroom and others will keep tighter control of your lessons. It is worth spending some time discussing with your mentor at the start of a period of school experience how they would like you to work with them.

Your mentor will be impressed if you go above and beyond the call of duty. You often only have limited time in schools to really showcase what you can do. It is up to you to make the most of this. Seek opportunities to support the wider life of the school by supporting the school's co-curriculum and volunteering to participate in events that are not compulsory. This demonstrates to your mentor that you are prepared to contribute to the team.

Mentors are busy people. They often have many additional responsibilities to undertake on top of their mentoring role. From the outset, agree with them when the best times are for you to meet with them, but be prepared to be flexible. Schools are complex organisations and things change frequently. Try not to expect to be 'spoon-fed' through your planning of lessons. It is acceptable in the earlier stages of your training to require greater guidance in relation to your lesson planning, but as you progress through your training, it is reasonable to expect that you will need less support. Go to meetings with ideas rather than expecting to be told what to do.

If the relationship breaks down with your mentor, you will need to talk to your ITT manager, tutor, lecturer or course leader. There may be various reasons why this has happened, and it may not be your fault. It is not the end of the world, and it will be resolved. Try to stay calm in difficult circumstances.

## 8.2 LEARNING FROM FEEDBACK

Your mentor will provide you with formal and informal feedback during your training. It is important to view feedback as a mechanism for developing you as a teacher rather than a mechanism for evaluating your performance. Effective feedback identifies strengths and areas for development in relation to your teaching. It is important for you to learn from all feedback by acting on the advice that you have been given.

Try to see feedback as a two-way conversation between you and your mentor rather than a one-way process. When you receive feedback on your teaching, be prepared to lead the conversation rather than passively waiting for your mentor to tell you how well you have done. Your mentor will also be trying to establish if you are reflective at the same time. Use feedback sessions as an opportunity for you to identify your own strengths and areas for development. Be prepared to take an active role during these meetings by asking questions and using the time to demonstrate that you can reflect on your own practice.

Actively pursue your own professional development by seeking opportunities to observe teachers across the school or by engaging in professional dialogue with colleagues. These are effective responses to the targets that your mentor provides. Seeking opportunities for team teaching or collaborative planning can also be effective strategies for acting on feedback. Acting on the targets that you have been set immediately will demonstrate to your mentor that you are committed to developing your skills and knowledge as a teacher.

## 8.3 REFLECTING ON YOUR DEVELOPMENT

Effective teachers are highly reflective and sometimes super-critical of themselves. Being overly critical of your performance is not good and is rarely an accurate appraisal of your teaching. Focus on what you are doing well and celebrate your strengths. You will have targets to address – all teachers have them. However, you may not be able to address them all at once. Decide which target is the most critical to your development as a teacher and work on improving that. Try to focus on what went well during your lessons and pick out one thing that you want to do better next time. You will be able to think of many things that you would like to improve, but just limit it to one target.

Don't punish yourself when you have a disastrous lesson. We all have them, including teachers who have been teaching for many years. Don't waste time and energy worrying about it. Instead, focus on what you need to do to improve the lesson so that the children can make better progress. Go back in the next day, reteach the lesson in a different way and ask your mentor to provide you with informal feedback. They will be impressed that you have adapted your teaching in response to the previous lesson.

Write evaluations of every lesson. These can be brief notes using bullet points to identify what went well and what needs to be improved. Make sure that you have identified more strengths than targets. You can even annotate your lesson plans with these notes. When you evaluate lessons, focus on children's progress as much as possible, as well as your own development as a teacher. Identify children who need additional support, and challenge and annotate your lesson plans to help you remember to address their needs in the next lesson.

Most reflection that you do will be through conversations with your mentor or other colleagues. You do not need to write everything down, but you do need to demonstrate actively that you are reflecting on your teaching through discussion. In addition, as well as reflecting after your lessons, you should also be reflecting on your teaching during your lessons. Through questioning the children or through other forms of assessment, you will be able to identify those pupils who have developed misconceptions and those who need additional levels of challenge. Effective teachers can adapt their teaching 'on the spot' during the lesson to respond to pupils' needs. It is therefore critical that you view reflection as continual rather than as a process that only occurs after teaching has taken place. If you adopt this latter position, you will miss opportunities to enable children to make further progress during their lessons.

## 8.4 WORKING WITH TEACHING ASSISTANTS

It is important to ascertain whether the TAs you will be working alongside in your classroom are employed to support specific children or deployed for general classroom support. Evidence from research suggests that TAs should not be deployed as an informal teaching resource to support low-attaining pupils (Sharples et al., 2015). All children are entitled to high-quality teaching from a teacher. Often, TAs are deployed to support learners with special educational needs and disabilities. This limits their exposure to a teacher, fosters a culture of dependency, separates these pupils from their peers and results in them making less progress than pupils who are taught by teachers (Sharples et al., 2015). It is, therefore, important that children who struggle the most have as much time with the teacher as others (Sharples et al., 2015). You will need to ensure that you take responsibility for the education of all pupils.

Finding time to involve TAs in planning lessons is challenging to achieve but good practice. Often, TAs have in-depth knowledge of the children they are supporting and can offer valuable insights to support lesson planning. You will need to consider how you will find the time to brief them prior to lessons so that they have clarity about their role in specific lessons.

You will also need to consider how you will deploy TAs during times when you are directly teaching the whole class. Examples of deployment could include:

- Working with specific children, breaking the subject content down further
- Monitoring the behaviour of specific children
- Working with specific children who need to catch up
- Supporting you in lesson delivery

You will need to consider how you will deploy them during the main part of the lesson. Examples include:

- Working with specific children or a group
- Implementing tailored interventions with children
- Monitoring the learning of the rest of the class to allow you to work intensively with a specific group of pupils

You will then need to consider carefully how you will deploy them at the end of a lesson. One example of effective deployment at the end of lessons is to ask them to provide immediate intervention to specific pupils who demonstrated misconceptions during the lesson. In addition, you might ask them to undertake low-level marking to allow you to sum up the learning and bring the lesson to a close.

## 8.5 WORKING WITH OTHER COLLEAGUES

In addition to working with your mentor and TAs, you will work alongside colleagues in school who undertake specialist roles and responsibilities. They may include behaviour support workers, pastoral staff, the special educational needs coordinator, family-liaison workers, clerical, catering, cleaning and premises staff. Within small primary schools, it is difficult to escape from people and it is therefore crucial that you establish positive relationships with members of the wider school workforce.

Take the opportunity to talk to the special educational needs coordinator about their roles and responsibilities. Find out about the intervention programmes that operate across the school to support pupils with specific learning needs. In addition, ask for advice on how best to support pupils with special educational needs and/or disabilities in your class. Talk to the Designated Safeguarding Lead to learn the processes for reporting concerns and managing disclosures. The school will have a safeguarding policy, but meeting with colleagues to find out more information demonstrates to your mentor that you are interested and enthusiastic. If the school hosts specialist provision – for example, for children with autism – seek out opportunities to spend time working within this provision to further your knowledge.

## 8.6 MANAGING YOUR WORKLOAD

Teachers experience significant workloads related to their professional roles. The tasks are often not too difficult to complete. However, the sheer volume of work-related tasks can become overwhelming at times. You will have to learn to manage your workload by keeping on top of your daily tasks. Creating a simple list of daily tasks and sequencing these into an order of importance is an effective way of prioritising tasks. Set yourself strict deadlines in order to stick to these. Avoid agreeing to take on unnecessary tasks so that your workload does not become unmanageable. Discuss with your mentor ways of reducing workloads related to planning and marking. Many schools are now developing a strategic response to manage workload, particularly in relation to reducing unnecessary planning, assessment and data management. Find out how your school is addressing the issue of workload strategically. The key to managing workload is to stay organised and to keep on top of your commitments.

## 8.7 MANAGING YOUR TIME

Time is precious and easy to waste. Try to make the best use of your time in school to ensure that you maximise your productivity. Ways of managing your time include:

- Allocating specific tasks to be completed before and after the school day
- Marking work during lesson time where feasible
- Providing verbal feedback to children instead of written feedback
- Live marking work using a visualiser
- Planning how you will utilise your non-contact time
- Allocating specific periods of time for each task and sticking rigidly to these
- Realising and accepting that it is not possible to complete every task to perfection

- Utilising resources that are available in school rather than making your own
- Asking colleagues if they have resources that they can share with you

Do not waste time laminating resources that you intend to use only once. Also, if you intend to invest time in making resources, make sure that these resources can be used multiple times. Protect time for sleep, rest and relaxation as these are important for your well-being.

## 8.8 MANAGING YOUR WELL-BEING

Your physical, social and mental well-being are important. These aspects are not distinct but are interrelated. For example, improving your physical well-being can also improve your mental well-being, and developing social connections can improve your mental well-being.

It is important to connect with others and stay physically active during your blocks of school experience. You should aim to allocate some time during the week when you are not working on school-related tasks. It is also important to ensure that you get enough uninterrupted sleep and that you are eating the right foods that will provide you with slow-release energy. During the school day, it is important to eat regularly, stay hydrated and find time to visit the bathroom.

Take responsibility for looking after yourself. Teachers who are mentally healthy are well-positioned to thrive in the classroom.

## 8.9 USING RESEARCH

Your training provider should ensure that you can access the latest research related to teaching. You should be able to access research articles and books to support your development as a teacher. In addition, there is a wealth of material available on the internet and social media platforms, such as X, to provide rich opportunities for collaboration with other teachers. A wide range of organisations now provide teachers with access to the latest research evidence. These include:

- The Chartered College of Teaching: https://chartered.college/
- The Sutton Trust: www.suttontrust.com/
- Institute for Effective Education: www.beib.org.uk/
- National Foundation for Educational Research: www.nfer.ac.uk/publications-research/

## 8.10 PROFESSIONAL DEVELOPMENT

Effective trainee teachers take responsibility for their own professional development. Professional development is any activity that facilitates professional learning. It can include attending or participating in courses and meetings, but it is not restricted to this. Informal conversations in corridors and staffrooms often provide rich opportunities for professional learning. Participating in staff meetings and In-Service Training (INSET) days also provides valuable opportunities to further develop your knowledge and skills as a teacher. Visiting other people's classrooms and observing other teachers is one of the most effective ways of developing your knowledge. Arranging opportunities to visit other schools where there is good practice is also a powerful way of further developing yourself as a teacher. In addition, participating in online platforms such as X is invaluable, as this provides you with an opportunity to interact with thousands of teachers who will freely give advice and support. Joining professional organisations, such as the Chartered College for Teaching, is a fantastic way of keeping up to date with research and pedagogy. Seek out opportunities for professional development rather than waiting for opportunities to come to you.

## 8.11 MEETING YOUR SAFEGUARDING RESPONSIBILITIES

You have a legal duty to safeguard children from harm. It is important that you read the school's safeguarding policy and the Department for Education *Keeping Children Safe in Education 2023* (DfE, 2023). It is also essential that you meet with the Designated Safeguarding Lead/Officer so that you know how to address concerns about children's safety and manage disclosures effectively. If you have any safeguarding concerns about a child, you should speak to your mentor in the first instance. Do not ignore your gut feeling; if you feel that a child may be at risk, it is likely that this is accurate.

## 8.12 WORKING WITH PARENTS

It is important to develop positive relationships with parents. As a trainee, you will generally see parents at the beginning and end of the day. Always smile and let them see how much you love working with their children. Communicate the child's successes with parents regularly through e-mails, text messages or telephone calls. If you experience a challenging situation with a parent, take the advice of your mentor and ask for your mentor to accompany you if parents request a meeting with you. Most parents will liaise with the class teacher rather than you, but they may start to liaise with you when your teaching commitment increases. To support you in building effective relationships, it is also valuable to take opportunities to communicate with parents by participating in parents' evenings.

## 8.13 CONTRIBUTING TO THE WIDER LIFE OF THE SCHOOL

During block periods of school experience, you should volunteer to participate in a wide range of events so that you develop a realistic understanding of the role of a teacher. These may include participation in:

- Extra-curricular activities
- Parents' evenings
- Educational visits
- School productions and school celebration events
- Staff social events
- School music events

### TAKE 5

- Teaching is a profession, and it is therefore important to develop a professional persona.
- Ask for advice when you need it; people want to help.
- Work efficiently to manage your workload and create a daily to-do list.
- Access support from peers, friends, family and teachers on social media to help you get through difficult times.
- Look after your well-being. Sleep, eat and protect time for physical activity and relaxation.

## CLASSROOM EXAMPLE

James is a trainee teacher in a postgraduate programme. He demonstrates a highly professional approach when he meets his mentor to review his progress. He takes ownership of the meeting by identifying what is going well and what aspects of his practice he needs to improve. He takes samples of his planning to the meetings to demonstrate to his mentor how he plans for progression in children's learning. He also takes one or two examples of children's work to the meetings, which enables him to provide evidence of pupil progress. He asks questions and demonstrates how he has addressed previous mentor feedback on his teaching. He then rigorously pursues his own professional development by observing practice in other classrooms, engaging in discussions with other teachers on X and carrying out personal research.

## EXAMPLES OF WHAT GOOD PRACTICE IN TEACHING ASSISTANT DEPLOYMENT LOOKS LIKE IN THE CLASSROOM

TAs can be deployed to provide pre-teaching to specific children prior to lessons. This provides them with an opportunity to introduce children to subject-specific knowledge, concepts and skills before the lesson is taught.

During the time when the teacher is modelling subject-specific knowledge, concepts or skills, TAs can be deployed with specific children to break the subject content down further and to provide additional modelling of these.

Teachers can also identify specific children during lessons who have developed subject-specific misconceptions. TAs can be deployed to provide immediate intervention to these pupils.

## SUMMARY

This chapter has outlined teachers' roles and responsibilities in relation to personal and professional conduct, and the importance of upholding public trust and maintaining professional boundaries with pupils and parents. It has demonstrated that you will be required to work in partnership with a wide range of people, including mentors, TAs and parents, and that you should take responsibility for investing effort into establishing effective and professional relationships. Some practical considerations have been outlined to support you in identifying and overcoming any challenges that you may experience, and your duties in relation to safeguarding have been highlighted.

# CONCLUSION

This book has outlined the *ITT Core Content Framework*. It has emphasised the importance of demonstrating high expectations of all pupils, regardless of social background or other circumstances. When these are combined with effective pedagogical approaches that are responsive to individual needs, teachers can reduce gaps in attainment between different groups of learners.

This book has outlined several pedagogical approaches that have a positive impact on children's learning. These include spacing learning out over time with opportunities to revisit learning, high-quality modelling, questioning, and retrieval practice. In addition, teachers who have strong subject knowledge can make a significant positive impact on pupils' learning. This book has emphasised the importance of integrating assessment into lessons so that teachers can check pupils' understanding, and identify and respond to their misconceptions.

This book has provided you with comprehensive guidance on managing and supporting children's behaviour. We have emphasised that all behaviour is a form of communication and that in addition to 'managing' behaviour in the classroom, teachers also need to identify the underpinning factors that shape children's behaviour.

We have outlined strategies to support the effective deployment of teaching assistants in order to prevent a culture of dependency occurring. We have emphasised that all children have an entitlement to the same amount of teaching from a qualified teacher. Teaching assistants form part of a package of support for specific children, but they should never replace the teacher.

We have discussed the need to develop a professional identity. This includes managing workload, meeting deadlines, listening to and acting on advice and monitoring one's behaviour outside of school. Some trainee teachers develop a professional identity quickly, but others struggle to adapt to working in a professional context and studying on a professional course. This book has outlined the steps that you need to take to adapt to your professional identity.

Finally, we have emphasised that you should see yourself as a learner. This process of learning to be a teacher will not end when you complete your course of initial teacher education. Learning to be a teacher is a career-long process. Effective teachers are continually learning. They are reflective and willing to adapt their practice to make it more effective. They are not afraid to ask for support when they need it, and they have a deep knowledge of both their learners and their own strengths and areas for development.

# REFERENCES


Aldridge, JM and McChesney, K (2018) The relationships between school climate and adolescent mental health and wellbeing: A systematic literature review. *International Journal of Educational Research*, 88: 121–45.

Assessment Reform Group (2002) *Assessment for Learning: 10 Principles*. London: Assessment Reform Group.

Barenberg, J, Roeder, U and Dutke, S (2018) Students' temporal distributing of learning activities in psychology courses: Factors of influence and effects on the metacognitive learning outcome. *Psychology Learning and Teaching*, 17 (3): 257–71.

Bjork, EL and Bjork, RA (2011) Making things hard on yourself, but in a good way: Creating desirable difficulties to enhance learning. In MA Gernsbacher, RW Pew, LM Hough and JR Pomerantz (eds), *Psychology and the Real World: Essays Illustrating Fundamental Contributions to Society* (56–64), New York, NY: Worth Publishers.

Black, P and Wiliam, D (1998) Inside the black box: Raising standards through classroom assessment. *Phi Delta Kappan*, 92 (1).

Bloom, BS (1956) *Taxonomy of Educational Objectives: The Classification of Educational Goals*. Philadelphia, PA: David McKay Company.

Cantor, P, Osher, D, Berg, J, Steyer, L and Rose, T (2019) Malleability, plasticity, and individuality: How children learn and develop in context. *Applied Developmental Science*, 23 (4): 307–37.

Carter, A (2015) *Carter Review of Initial Teacher Training (ITT)*. London: DfE.

Coe, R, Aloisi, C, Higgins, S and Elliot Major, L (2014) *What Makes Great Teaching?* London: The Sutton Trust.

Condie, R, Livingston, K and Seagraves, L (2005) *Evaluation of the Assessment for Learning Programme: Final Report*. Glasgow: Quality in Education Centre, University of Strathclyde.

Creemers, BPM and Kyriakides, L (2006) Critical analysis of the current approaches to modelling educational effectiveness: The importance of establishing a dynamic model. *School Effectiveness and School Improvement*, 17: 347–66.

Darling-Hammond, L, Flook, L, Cook-Harvey, C, Barron, B and Osher, D (2019) Implications for educational practice of the science of learning and development. *Applied Developmental Science*, 1–44.

Department for Education (DfE) (2011) *Teachers' Standards Guidance for School Leaders, School Staff and Governing Bodies*. London: DfE.

Department for Education (DfE) (2013) *The National Curriculum in England*. London: DfE.

Department for Education (DfE) (2019a) *Early Career Framework*. London: DfE.

Department for Education (DfE) (2019b) *School Workload Reduction Toolkit*. London: DfE.

Department for Education (DfE) (2023) *Keeping Children Safe in Education 2023*. London: DfE.

Department for Education (DfE) and Department of Health (DoH) (2015) *Special Educational Needs and Disability Code of Practice: 0 to 25 Years Statutory Guidance for Organisations Which Work with and Support Children and Young People Who Have Special Educational Needs or Disabilities*. London: DfE/DoH.

Department for Education (DfE) and Education Endowment Foundation (EEF) (2019) *ITT Core Content Framework*. London: DfE/EEF.

Education Endowment Foundation (2021), *Cognitive Science Approaches in the Classroom: A Review of the Evidence*. London: EEF.

Farrington, CA, Roderick, M, Allensworth, E, Nagaoka, J, Keyes, TS, Johnson, DW and Beechum, NO (2012) *Teaching Adolescents to become Learners: The Role of Noncognitive Factors in Shaping School Performance: A Critical Literature Review*. Chicago, IL: University of Chicago Consortium on Chicago School Research.

Flórez, MT and Sammons, P (2013) *Assessment for Learning: Effects and Impact*. Berkshire: CfBT Education Trust.

Francis, B, Archer, L, Hodgen, J, Pepper, D, Taylor, B and Travers, M (2017) Exploring the relative lack of impact of research on 'ability grouping' in England: A discourse analytic account. *Cambridge Journal of Education*, 47 (1): 1–17.

Georghiades, P (2004) From the general to the situated: Three decades of metacognition. *International Journal of Science Education*, 26 (3): 365–83.

Gipps, C, McCallum, B, Hargreaves, E and Pickering, A (2005) From TA to assessment for learning: The impact of assessment policy on teachers' assessment practice. Paper presented at the *British Educational Research Association Annual Conference*, University of Glamorgan, 14–17, September 2005.

Harding, S, Morris, R, Gunnella, D, Ford, T et al. (2019) Is teachers' mental health and wellbeing associated with students' mental health and wellbeing? *Journal of Affective Disorders*, 242: 180–7.

Hart, S, Dixon, A, Drummond, MJ and McIntyre, D (2004) *Learning without Limits*. Maidenhead: Open University Press.

Hattie, J and Timperley, H (2007) The power of feedback. *Review of Educational Research*, 77 (1): 81–112.

Higgins, S, Katsipataki, M, Kokotsaki, D, Coleman, R, Major, LE and Coe, R (2014) *The Sutton Trust-Education Endowment Foundation Teaching and Learning Toolkit*. London: Education Endowment Foundation.

Ireson, J (1999) *Innovative Grouping Practices in Secondary Schools*. Research Report, No. 166. Available online at: http://dera.ioe.ac.uk/4460/1/RR166.pdf

Jennings, PA and Greenberg, MT (2009) The prosocial classroom: Teacher social and emotional competence in relation to student and classroom outcomes. *Review of Educational Research*, 79 (1): 491–525.

Kellard, K, Costello, M, Godfrey, D, Griffiths, E and Rees, C (2008) *Evaluation of the Developing Thinking and Assessment for Learning Development Programme*. Welsh Assembly Government.

Kidger, J, Araya, R, Donovan, J and Gunnell, D (2012) The effect of the school environment on the emotional health of adolescents: A systematic review. *Pediatrics*, 129 (5): 2011–248.

Kidger, J, Gunnell, D, Biddle, L, Campbell, R and Donovan, J (2010) Part and parcel of teaching? Secondary school staff's views on supporting student emotional health and well-being. *British Educational Research Journal*, 36 (6): 919–35.

Kirton, A, Hallam, S, Peffers, J, Robertson, P and Stobart, G (2007) Revolution, evolution or a Trojan horse? Piloting assessment for learning in some Scottish secondary schools. *British Educational Research Journal*, 33 (4), 605–27.

MacPhail, A and Halbert, J (2010) 'We had to do intelligent thinking during recent PE': Students' and teachers' experiences of assessment for learning in post-secondary physical education. *Assessment in Education: Principles, Policy and Practice*, 17 (1): 23–39.

Maslow, AH (1943) A theory of human motivation. Psychological Review, 50 (4), 370–396.

Maslow, AH (1948) 'Higher' and 'lower' needs. *The Journal of Psychology: Interdisciplinary and Applied*, 25: 433–6. Available online at: https://doi.org/10.1080/00223980.1948.9917386

Moore, DS (2015) *The Developing Genome: An Introduction to Behavioral Epigenetics*. New York, NY: Oxford University Press.

National Education Union (NEU) (2021) *Turning the Page on Poverty: A Practical Guide for Education Staff to Help Tackle Poverty and the Cost of the School Day*. NEU.

Office for Standards in Education, Children's Services and Skills (Ofsted) (2019a) *The Education Inspection Framework*. Available online at: https://www.gov.uk/government/publications/education-inspection-framework/education-inspection-framework

Office for Standards in Education (Ofsted), (2019b) *Education Inspection Framework: Overview of Research*. Manchester: Ofsted.

Office for Standards in Education (Ofsted) (2021a) *Guidance: School Inspection Handbook*. Available online at: https://www.gov.uk/government/publications/school-inspection-handbook-eif/school-inspection-handbook

Office for Standards in Education (Ofsted) (2021b) *Research Review Series: Mathematics*. Available online at: https://www.gov.uk/government/publications/research-review-series-mathematics/research-review-series-mathematics

Office for Standards in Education (Ofsted) (2023) *School Inspection Handbook*. Available online at: https://www.gov.uk/government/publications/school-inspection-handbook-eif/school-inspection-handbook-for-september-2023

Plenty, S, Östberg, V, Almquist, YB, Augustine, L and Modin, B (2014) Psychosocial working conditions: An analysis of emotional symptoms and conduct problems amongst adolescent students. *Journal of Adolescence*, 37 (4): 407–17.

Rawson, KA and Kintsch, W (2005) Rereading effects depend on time of test. *Journal of Educational Psychology*, 97 (1): 70–80. https://doi.org/10.1037/0022-0663.97.1.70

Roediger, H and Karpicke, J (2006) Test-enhanced learning. *Psychological Science*, 17 (3): 249–55.

Rose, J (2006) *Rose Report: Independent Review of the Teaching of Early Reading*. London: DfES.

Rosenshine, B (2010) *Principles of Instruction*. International Academy of Education, UNESCO. Geneva: International Bureau of Education. Available online at: www.ibe.unesco.org/fileadmin/user_upload/Publications/Educational_Practices/EdPractices_21.pdf

Rosenshine, B (2012) Principles of instruction: Research based principles that all teachers should know. *American Educator*, Spring. Available online at: www.aft.org/pdfs/american-educator/spring2012/Rosenshine.pdf

Sharples, J, Webster, R and Blatchford, P (2015) *Making Best Use of Teaching Assistants: Guidance Report*. London: Education Endowment Foundation.

Skinner, BF (1938) *The Behaviour of Organisms: An Experimental Analysis*. New York, NY: Appleton-Century.

Slavich, GM and Cole, SW (2013) The emerging field of human social genomics. *Clinical Psychological Science*, 1 (3): 331–48.

Slavin, RE (1987) Ability grouping and student achievement in elementary schools: A best-evidence synthesis. *Review of Educational Research*, 57 (3): 293–336.

Slavin, RE (1990) Achievement effects of ability grouping in secondary schools: A best-evidence synthesis. *Review of Educational Research*, 60: 471–99.

Steenbergen-Hu, S, Makel, MC and Olszewski-Kubilius, P (2016) What one hundred years of research says about the effects of ability grouping and acceleration on K–12 students' academic achievement. *Review of Educational Research*, 86 (4): 849–99.

Stipek, D, Newton, S and Chudgar, A (2010) Learning-related behaviors and literacy achievement in elementary school-aged children. *Early Childhood Research Quarterly*, 25 (3): 385–95.

Sweller, J, Ayres, P and Kalyuga, S (2011) *Cognitive Load Theory: Volume 1*. New York, NY: Springer.

Taylor, B, Francis, B, Archer, L, Hodgen, J, Pepper, D, Tereshchenko, A and Travers, M (2016) Factors deterring schools from mixed attainment teaching practice. *Pedagogy, Culture and Society*, 25 (3).

Tomlinson, CA (2000) Differentiation of instruction in the elementary grades. In *ERIC Digests*. Syracuse, NY: Office of Educational Research and Improvement (ED), Washington, DC.

Torrance, H and Pryor, J (2001) Developing formative assessment in the classroom: Using action research to explore and modify theory. *British Educational Research Journal*, 27 (5): 615–31.

Webb, M and Jones, J (2009) Exploring tensions in developing assessment for learning. *Assessment in Education*, 16 (2): 165–84.

# FURTHER READING

Source: The Department for Education and Education Endowment Foundation (DfE/EEF) (2019) *The ITT Core Content Framework*. Manchester: DfE. Crown copyright.

## HIGH EXPECTATIONS (STANDARD 1 – 'SET HIGH EXPECTATIONS')

*[Further reading recommendations are indicated with an asterisk.]*


Aronson, J. (Ed.) (2002) *Improving Academic Achievement: Impact of Psychological Factors on Education*. New York, NY: Academic Press.

Bandura, A. (1986) *Social Foundations of Thought and Action: A Social Cognitive Theory*. Englewood Cliffs, NJ: Prentice-Hall.

Campbell Collaboration (2018) School-based interventions for reducing disciplinary school exclusion. *A Systematic Review*. Accessible from: https://campbellcollaboration.org/library/reducing-school-exclusion-school-based-interventions.html

Chapman, R. L., Buckley, L., & Sheehan, M. (2013) School-Based programs for increasing connectedness and reducing risk behavior. *A Systematic Review*, 25(1), 95–114.

Chetty, R., Friedman, J. N., Rockoff, J. E. (2014) Measuring the impacts of teachers II: Teacher value-added and student outcomes in adulthood. *The American Economic Review*, 104(9), 2633–2679. https://doi.org/10.1257/aer.104.9.2633

*Education Endowment Foundation (2018) *Sutton Trust-Education Endowment Foundation Teaching and Learning Toolkit*. Accessible from: https://educationendowmentfoundation.org.uk/evidence-summaries/teaching-learning-toolkit [retrieved 10 October 2018].

Hanushek, E. (1992) The trade-off between child quantity and quality. *Journal of Political Economy*, 100(4), 859–887.

*Institute of Education Sciences (2008) *Reducing Behavior Problems in the Elementary School Classroom*. Accessible from: https://ies.ed.gov/ncee/wwc/PracticeGuide/4

Johnson, S., Buckingham, M., Morris, S., Suzuki, S., Weiner, M., Hershberg, R., B. Weiner, Hershberg, R., Fremont, E., Batanova, M., Aymong, C., Hunter, C., Bowers, E., Lerner, J., & Lerner, R. (2016) Adolescents' character role models: Exploring who young people look up to as examples of how to be a good person. *Research in Human Development*, 13(2), 126–141. https://doi.org/10.1080/15427609.2016.1164552

Jussim, L., & Harber, K. (2005) Teacher expectations and self-fulfilling prophecies: Knowns and unknowns, resolved and unresolved controversies. *Personality and Social Psychology Review*, 9(2), 131–155.

Lazowski, R. A., & Hulleman, C. S. (2016) Motivation interventions in education: A meta-analytic review. *Review of Educational Research*, 86(2), 602–640. https://doi.org/10.3102/0034654315617832

Murdock-Perriera, L. A., & Sedlacek, Q. C. (2018) Questioning Pygmalion in the twenty-first century: The formation, transmission, and attributional influence of teacher expectancies. *Social Psychology of Education*, 21(3), 691–707. https://doi.org/10.1007/s11218-018-9439-9

*PISA (2015) PISA in Focus: Do teacher-student relations affect students' well-being at school? https://doi.org/10.1787/22260919

Rathmann K., Herke M., Hurrelmann K., & Richter M. (2018) Perceived class climate and school-aged children's life satisfaction: The role of the learning environment in classrooms. *PLoS One*, 13(2), e0189335. https://doi.org/10.1371/journal.pone.0189335

Rubie-Davies, C. M., Weinstein, R. S., Huang, F. L., Gregory, A., Cowan, P. A., & Cowan, C. P. (2014) Successive teacher expectation effects across the early school years. *Journal of Applied Developmental Psychology*, 35(3), 181–191. https://doi.org/10.1016/j.appdev.2014.03.006

Slater, H., Davies, N. M., & Burgess, S. (2011) Do teachers matter? Measuring the variation in teacher effectiveness in England. *Oxford Bulletin of Economics and Statistics*. https://doi.org/10.1111/j.1468-0084.2011.00666.x

Tsiplakides, I., & Keramida, A. (2010) The relationship between teacher expectations and student achievement in the teaching of English as a foreign language. *English Language Teaching*, 3(2), P22. Accessible from: http://files.eric.ed.gov/fulltext/EJ1081569.pdf

Wubbels, T., Brekelmans, M., den Brok, P., Wijsman, L., Mainhard, T., & van Tartwijk, J. (2014) Teacher-student relationships and classroom management. In E. T. Emmer, E. Sabornie, C. Evertson, & C. Weinstein (Eds.). *Handbook of Classroom Management: Research, Practice, and Contemporary Issues* (2nd ed., pp. 363–386). New York, NY: Routledge.

Zins, J. E., Bloodworth, M. R., Weissberg, R. P., & Walberg, H. J. (2007) The scientific base linking social and emotional learning to school success. *Journal of Educational and Psychological Consultation*, 17(2–3), 191–210. https://doi.org/10.1080/10474410701413145

## HOW PUPILS LEARN (STANDARD 2 – 'PROMOTE GOOD PROGRESS')

*[Further reading recommendations are indicated with an asterisk.]*

Adesope, O. O., Trevisan, D. A., & Sundararajan, N. (2017) Rethinking the use of tests: A meta-analysis of practice testing. *Review of Educational Research*, 87(3), 659–701. https://doi.org/10.3102/0034654316689306

Agarwal, P. K., Finley, J. R., Rose, N. S., & Roediger, H. L. (2017) Benefits from retrieval practice are greater for students with lower working memory capacity. *Memory*, 25(6), 764–771. https://doi.org/10.1080/09658211.2016.1220579

Allen, B., & Sims, S. (2018) *The Teacher Gap*. Abingdon: Routledge.

Baddeley, A. (2003) Working memory: Looking back and looking forward. *Nature Reviews Neuroscience*, 4(10), 829–839.

Black, P., & Wiliam, D. (2009) Developing the theory of formative assessment. *Educational Assessment, Evaluation and Accountability*, 21(1), 5–31.

Chi, M. T. (2009) Three types of conceptual change: Belief revision, mental model transformation, and categorical shift. In *International Handbook of Research on Conceptual Change* (pp. 89–110). New York, NY and London: Routledge.

Clark, R., Nguyen, F., & Sweller, J. (2006) *Efficiency in Learning: Evidence-Based Guidelines to Manage Cognitive Load*. San Francisco, CA: John Wiley & Sons.

Cowan, N. (2008) What are the differences between long-term, short-term, and working memory? *Progress in Brain Research*, 169, 323–338.

*Deans for Impact (2015) The Science of Learning. Accessible from: https://deansforimpact.org/resources/the-science-oflearning/ [retrieved 10 October 2018].

Dunlosky, J., Rawson, K. A., Marsh, E. J., Nathan, M. J., & Willingham, D. T. (2013) Improving students' learning with effective learning techniques: Promising directions from cognitive and educational psychology. *Psychological Science in the Public Interest, Supplement*, 14(1), 4–58. https://doi.org/10.1177/1529100612453266

*Education Endowment Foundation (2018) Improving Secondary Science Guidance Report. Accessible from: https://educationendowmentfoundation.org.uk/tools/guidance-reports/ [retrieved 10 October 2018].

Gathercole, S., Lamont, E., & Alloway, T. (2006) Working memory in the classroom. *Working memory and education*, 219–240.

Hattie, J. (2012) *Visible Learning for Teachers*. Oxford: Routledge.

Kirschner, P., Sweller, J., Kirschner, F., & Zambrano, J. (2018) From cognitive load theory to collaborative cognitive load theory. *International Journal of Computer-Supported Collaborative Learning*, 13(2), 213–233.

Pachler, H., Bain, P. M., Bottge, B. A., Graesser, A., Koedinger, K., McDaniel, M., & Metcalfe, J. (2007) *Organizing Instruction and Study to Improve Student Learning*. Washington, DC: US Department of Education.

Pan, S. C., & Rickard, T. C. (2018) Transfer of test-enhanced learning: Meta-analytic review and synthesis. *Psychological Bulletin*, 144(7), 710–756. https://doi.org/10.1037/bul0000151

Roediger, H. L., & Butler, A. C. (2011) The critical role of retrieval practice in long-term retention. *Trends in Cognitive Sciences*, 15(1), 20–27. https://doi.org/10.1016/j.tics.2010.09.003

*Rosenshine, B. (2012) Principles of Instruction: Research-based strategies that all teachers should know. *American Educator*, 12–20. https://doi.org/10.1111/j.1467-8535.2005.00507.x

Simonsmeier, B. A., Flaig, M., Deiglmayr, A., Schalk, L., & Well-being, S. (2018) Domain-Specific Prior Knowledge and Learning: A Meta-Analysis Prior Knowledge and Learning. Accessible from: https://www.psycharchives.org/handle/20.500.12034/642

Sweller, J. (2016). Working memory, long-term memory, and instructional design. *Journal of Applied Research in Memory and Cognition*, 5(4), 360–367. http://doi.org/10.1016/j.jarmac.2015.12.002

Willingham, D. T. (2009) *Why Don't Students Like School?* San Francisco, CA: Jossey-Bass.

Wittwer, J., & Renkl, A. (2010) How effective are instructional explanations in example-based learning? A meta-analytic review. *Educational Psychology Review*, 22(4), 393–409. https://doi.org/10.1007/s10648-010-9136-5

## SUBJECT AND CURRICULUM (STANDARD 3 – 'DEMONSTRATE GOOD SUBJECT AND CURRICULUM KNOWLEDGE')

*[Further reading recommendations are indicated with an asterisk.]*

Bailin, S., Case, R., Coombs, J. R., & Daniels, L. B. (1999) Common misconceptions of critical thinking. *Journal of Curriculum Studies*, 31(3), 269–283.

Ball, D. L., Thames, M. H., & Phelps, G. (2008) Content knowledge for teachers: What makes it special? *Journal of Teacher Education*, 59, 389. https://doi.org/10.1177/0022487108324554 Accessible from: https://www.math.ksu.edu/~bennett/onlinehw/qcenter/ballmkt.pdf

Biesta, G. (2009) Good education in an age of measurement: On the need to reconnect with the question of purpose in education. *Educational Assessment, Evaluation and Accountability*, 21(1).

*Coe, R., Aloisi, C., Higgins, S., & Major, L. E. (2014) *What Makes Great Teaching. Review of the Underpinning Research.* Durham University. Accessible from: http://bit.ly/2OvmvKO

Cowan, N. (2008) What are the differences between long-term, short-term, and working memory? *Progress in Brain Research*, 169, 323–338.

Deans for Impact (2015) The Science of Learning. Accessible from: https://deansforimpact.org/resources/the-science-oflearning/ [retrieved 10 October 2018].

Education Endowment Foundation (2018) Improving Secondary Science Guidance Report. Accessible from: https://educationendowmentfoundation.org.uk/tools/guidance-reports/ [retrieved 10 October 2018].

Education Endowment Foundation (2018) Preparing for Literacy Guidance Report. Accessible from: https://educationendowmentfoundation.org.uk/public/files/Preparing_Literacy_Guidance_ 2018.pdf

Education Endowment Foundation (2018) Sutton Trust-Education Endowment Foundation Teaching and Learning Toolkit. Accessible from: https://educationendowmentfoundation.org.uk/evidence-summaries/teaching-learning-toolkit/ [retrieved 10 October 2018].

Guzzetti, B. J. (2000) Learning counter-intuitive science concepts: What have we learned from over a decade of research? *Reading & Writing Quarterly: Overcoming Learning Difficulties*, 16, 89–98. http://dx.doi.org/10.1080/105735600277971

Jerrim, J., & Vignoles, A. (2016) The link between East Asian "mastery" teaching methods and English children's mathematics skills. *Economics of Education Review*, 50, 29–44. https://doi.org/10.1016/j.econedurev.2015.11.003

Machin, S., McNally, S., & Viarengo, M. (2018) Changing how literacy is taught: Evidence on synthetic phonics. *American Economic Journal: Economic Policy*, 10(2), 217–241. https://doi.org/10.1257/pol.20160514

Rich, P. R., Van Loon, M. H., Dunlosky, J., & Zaragoza, M. S. (2017) Belief in corrective feedback for common misconceptions: Implications for knowledge revision. *Journal of Experimental Psychology: Learning, Memory, and Cognition*, 43(3), 492–501. http://dx.doi.org/10.1037/xlm0000322

*Rosenshine, B. (2012) Principles of Instruction: Research-based strategies that all teachers should know. *American Educator*, 12–20. Accessible from: https://www.aft.org//sites/default/files/periodicals/Rosenshine.pdf

Scott, C. E., McTigue, E. M., Miller, D. M., & Washburn, E. K. (2018) The what, when, and how of preservice teachers and literacy across the disciplines/: A systematic literature review of nearly 50 years of research. *Teaching and Teacher Education*, 73, 1–13. https://doi.org/10.1016/j.tate.2018.03.010

*Shanahan, T. (2005) The National Reading Panel Report: Practical Advice for Teachers. Accessible from: https://files.eric.ed.gov/fulltext/ED489535.pdf

Sweller, J., van Merrienboer, J. J. G., & Paas, F. G. W. C. (1998) Cognitive architecture and instructional design. *Educational Psychology Review*, 10(3), 251–296. https://doi.org/10.1023/A:1022193728205

Willingham, D. T. (2002) Ask the cognitive scientist. Inflexible knowledge: The first step to expertise. *American Educator*, 26(4), 31–33. Accessible from: https://www.aft.org/periodical/american-educator/winter-2002/ask-cognitive-scientist

## CLASSROOM PRACTICE (STANDARD 4 – 'PLAN AND TEACH WELL-STRUCTURED LESSONS')

*[Further reading recommendations are indicated with an asterisk.]*

Alexander, R. (2017) *Towards Dialogic Teaching: Rethinking Classroom Talk*. York: Dialogos.

*Coe, R., Aloisi, C., Higgins, S., & Major, L. E. (2014) *What Makes Great Teaching. Review of the Underpinning Research*. Durham University. Accessible from: http://bit.ly/2OvmvKO

Donker, A. S., de Boer, H., Kostons, D., Dignath van Ewijk, C. C., & van der Werf, M. P. C. (2014) Effectiveness of learning strategy instruction on academic performance: A meta-analysis. *Educational Research Review*, 11, 1–26. https://doi.org/10.1016/j.edurev.2013.11.002

Donovan, M. S., & Bransford, J. D. (2005) *How Students Learn: Mathematics in the Classroom*. Washington, DC: The National Academies Press.

Dunlosky, J., Rawson, K. A., Marsh, E. J., Nathan, M. J., & Willingham, D. T. (2013) Improving students' learning with effective learning techniques: Promising directions from cognitive and educational psychology. *Psychological Science in the Public Interest, Supplement*, 14(1), 4–58. https://doi.org/10.1177/1529100612453266

Education Endowment Foundation (2016) Improving Literacy in Key Stage One Guidance Report. Accessible from: https://educationendowmentfoundation.org.uk/tools/guidance-reports/ [retrieved 10 October 2018].

Education Endowment Foundation (2017) Improving Mathematics in Key Stages Two and Three Guidance Report. Accessible from: https://educationendowmentfoundation.org.uk/tools/guidance-reports/ [retrieved 10 October 2018].

Education Endowment Foundation (2017) Metacognition and Self-Regulated Learning Guidance Report. Accessible from: https://educationendowmentfoundation.org.uk/tools/guidance-reports/ [retrieved 10 October 2018].

Education Endowment Foundation (2018) Improving Secondary Science Guidance Report. Accessible from: https://educationendowmentfoundation.org.uk/tools/guidance-reports/ [retrieved 10 October 2018].

*Education Endowment Foundation (2018) Sutton Trust-Education Endowment Foundation Teaching and Learning Toolkit. Accessible from: https://educationendowmentfoundation.org.uk/evidence-summaries/teaching-learning-toolkit/ [retrieved 10 October 2018].

Elleman, A. M., Lindo, E. J., Morphy, P., & Compton, D. L. (2009) The impact of vocabulary instruction on passage-level comprehension of school-age children: A meta-analysis. *Journal of Research on Educational Effectiveness*, 2(1), 1–44. https://doi.org/10.1080/19345740802539200

Hodgen, J., Foster, C., Marks, R., & Brown, M. (2018) Improving Mathematics in Key Stages Two and Three: Evidence Review. Accessible from: https://educationendowmentfoundation.org.uk/evidence-summaries/evidence-reviews/improvingmathematics-in-key-stages-two-and-three/ [retrieved 22 October 2018].

Institute of Education Sciences (2009) Assisting Students Struggling with Mathematics: Response to Intervention for Elementary and Middle Schools. Accessible from: https://ies.ed.gov/ncee/wwc/Docs/PracticeGuide/rti_math_pg_042109.pdf

Jay, T., Willis, B., Thomas, P., Taylor, R., Moore, N., Burnett, C., Merchant, G., & Stevens, A. (2017) Dialogic Teaching: Evaluation Report. Accessible from: https://educationendowmentfoundation.org.uk/projects-and-evaluation/projects/dialogicteaching [retrieved 10 October 2018].

Kalyuga, S. (2007) Expertise reversal effect and its implications for learner-tailored instruction. *Educational Psychology Review*, 19(4), 509–539.

Kirschner, P., Sweller, J., Kirschner, F., & Zambrano, J. (2018) From cognitive load theory to collaborative cognitive load theory. *International Journal of Computer-Supported Collaborative Learning*, 13(2), 213–233.

Leung, K. C. (2015) Preliminary empirical model of crucial determinants of best practice for peer tutoring on academic achievement. *Journal of Educational Psychology*, 107(2), 558–579. https://doi.org/10.1037/a0037698

Muijs, D., & Reynolds, D. (2017) *Effective Teaching: Evidence and Practice.* Thousand Oaks, CA: SAGE.

Pan, S. C., & Rickard, T. C. (2018) Transfer of test-enhanced learning: Meta-analytic review and synthesis. *Psychological Bulletin*, 144(7), 710–756. Accessible from: http://psycnet.apa.org/doiLanding?doi=10.1037%2Fbul0000151

*Rosenshine, B. (2012) Principles of Instruction: Research-based strategies that all teachers should know. *American Educator*, 12–20. https://doi.org/10.1111/j.1467-8535.2005.00507.x

Sweller, J. (2016) Working memory, long-term memory, and instructional design. *Journal of Applied Research in Memory and Cognition*, 5(4), 360–367. http://doi.org/10.1016/j.jarmac.2015.12.002

Tereshchenko, A., Francis, B., Archer, L., Hodgen, J., Mazenod, A., Taylor, B., & Travers, M. C. (2018) Learners' attitudes to mixed-attainment grouping: Examining the views of students of high, middle and low attainment. *Research Papers in Education*, 1522, 1–20. https://doi.org/10.1080/02671522.2018.1452962

Van de Pol, J., Volman, M., Oort, F., & Beishuizen, J. (2015) The effects of scaffolding in the classroom: Support contingency and student independent working time in relation to student achievement, task effort and appreciation of support. *Instructional Science*, 43(5), 615–641.

Wittwer, J., & Renkl, A. (2010) How effective are instructional explanations in example-based learning? A meta-analytic review. *Educational Psychology Review*, 22(4), 393–409. https://doi.org/10.1007/s10648-010-9136-5

Zimmerman, B. J. (2002) Becoming a self-regulated learner: An overview, theory into practice. *Theory into Practice*, 41(2), 64–70. Accessible from: https://www.jstor.org/stable/1477457?seq=1#page_scan_tab_contents

## ADAPTIVE TEACHING (STANDARD 5 – 'ADAPT TEACHING')

*[Further reading recommendations are indicated with an asterisk.]*

*Davis, P., Florian, L., Ainscow, M., Dyson, A., Farrell, P., Hick, P., & Rouse, M. (2004) Teaching Strategies and Approaches for Pupils with Special Educational Needs: A Scoping Study. Accessible from: http://dera.ioe.ac.uk/6059/1/RR516.pdf

Deunk, M. I., Smale-Jacobse, A. E., de Boer, H., Doolaard, S., & Bosker, R. J. (2018) Effective differentiation practices: A systematic review and meta-analysis of studies on the cognitive effects of differentiation practices in primary education. *Educational Research Review*, 24(February), 31–54. https://doi.org/10.1016/j.edurev.2018.02.002

*Education Endowment Foundation (2018) Sutton Trust-Education Endowment Foundation Teaching and Learning Toolkit. Accessible from: https://educationendowmentfoundation.org.uk/evidence-summaries/teaching-learning-toolkit [retrieved 10 October 2018].

Hattie, J. (2009) *Visible Learning: A Synthesis of over 800 Meta-Analyses Relating to Achievement.* London: Routledge.

Kriegbaum, K., Becker, N., & Spinath, B. (2018) The relative importance of intelligence and motivation as predictors of school achievement: A meta-analysis. *Educational Research Review.* https://doi.org/10.1016/j.edurev.2018.10.001

*OECD (2015) Pisa 2015 Result: Policies and Practices for Successful Schools. https://doi.org/10.1787/9789264267510-en

Pashler, H., McDaniel, M., Rohrer, D., & Bjork, R. (2008) Learning styles: Concepts and evidence. *Psychological Science in the Public Interest*, 9(3).

Sisk, V. F., Burgoyne, A. P., Sun, J., Butler, J. L., & Macnamara, B. N. (2018) To what extent and under which circumstances are growth mind-sets important to academic achievement? Two meta-analyses. *Psychological Science*, 29(4), 549–571. https://doi.org/10.1177/0956797617739704

Speckesser, S., Runge, J., Foliano, F., Bursnall, M., Hudson-Sharp, N., Rolfe, H., & Anders, J. (2018) Embedding Formative Assessment: Evaluation Report. Accessible from: https://educationendowmentfoundation.org.uk/public/files/EFA_evaluation_report.pdf [retrieved 10 October 2018].

Steenbergen-Hu, S., Makel, M. C., & Olszewski-Kubilius, P. (2016) What one hundred years of research says about the effects of ability grouping and acceleration on K-12 students academic achievement: Findings of two second-order meta-analyses. *Review of Educational Research*,86. https://doi.org/10.3102/0034654316675417

Tereshchenko, A., Francis, B., Archer, L., Hodgen, J., Mazenod, A., Taylor, B., & Travers, M. C. (2018) Learners' attitudes to mixed-attainment grouping: Examining the views of students of high, middle and low attainment. *Research Papers in Education*, 1522, 1–20. https://doi.org/10.1080/02671522.2018.1452962

Willingham, D. T. (2010) The myth of learning styles, *Change*, 42(5), 32–35.

## ASSESSMENT (STANDARD 6 – 'MAKE ACCURATE AND PRODUCTIVE USE OF ASSESSMENT')

*[Further reading recommendations are indicated with an asterisk.]*

Black, P., & Wiliam, D. (2009) Developing the theory of formative assessment. *Educational Assessment, Evaluation and Accountability*, 21(1), 5–31.

*Black, P., Harrison, C., Lee, C., Marshall, B., & Wiliam, D. (2004). Working inside the black box: Assessment for learning in the classroom. *Phi Delta Kappan*, 86(1), 8–21. Accessible from: https://eric.ed.gov/?id=EJ705962

Christodoulou, D. (2017) *Making Good Progress: The Future of Assessment for Learning*. Oxford: OUP.

*Coe, R. (2013) *Improving Education: A Triumph of Hope over Experience*. Centre for Evaluation and Monitoring. Accessible from: http://www.cem.org/attachments/publications/ImprovingEducation2013.pdf

*Education Endowment Foundation (2016) A Marked Improvement? A Review of the Evidence on Written Marking. Accessible from: https://educationendowmentfoundation.org.uk/public/files/Publications/EEF_Marking_Review_April_2016.pdf

Education Endowment Foundation (2018) Sutton Trust-Education Endowment Foundation Teaching and Learning Toolkit: Accessible from: https://educationendowmentfoundation.org.uk/evidence-summaries/teaching-learning-toolkit/ [retrieved 10 October 2018].

Gibson, S., Oliver, L., & Dennison, M. (2015) *Workload Challenge: Analysis of Teacher Consultation Responses*. Department for Education. Accessible from: https://assets.publishing.service.gov.uk/government/uploads/system/uploads/attachment_data/file/485075/DFE-RR456A_-_Workload_Challenge_Analysis_of_teacher_consultation_responses_sixth_form_colleges.pdf

Hattie, J., & Timperley, H. (2007) The power of feedback. *Review of Educational Research*, 77(1), 81–112. https://doi.org/10.3102/003465430298487

Harlen, W., & James, M. (1997) Assessment and learning: Differences and relationships between formative and summative assessment, assessment in education: Principles, *Policy & Practice*, 4(3), 365–379.

Kluger, A. N., & DeNisi, A. (1996) The effects of feedback interventions on performance: A historical review, a meta-analysis, and a preliminary feedback intervention theory. *Psychological Bulletin*, 119(2), 254–284. https://doi.org/10.1037/0033-2909.119.2.254

Sadler, D. (1989) Formative assessment and the design of instructional systems. *Instructional Science*, 18(2), 119–144.

Speckesser, S., Runge, J., Foliano, F., Bursnall, M., Hudson-Sharp, N., Rolfe, H., & Anders, J. (2018) Embedding Formative Assessment: Evaluation Report. Accessible from: https://educationendowmentfoundation.org.uk/public/files/EFA_evaluation_report.pdf [retrieved 10 October 2018].

Wiliam, D. (2010) What counts as evidence of educational achievement? The role of constructs in the pursuit of equity in assessment. *Review of Research in Education*, 34, 254–284.

Wiliam, D. (2017) Assessment, marking and feedback. In Hendrick, C., & McPherson, R. (Eds.). *What Does This Look like in the Classroom? Bridging the Gap between Research and Practice*. Woodbridge: John Catt.

## MANAGING BEHAVIOUR (STANDARD 7 – 'MANAGE BEHAVIOUR EFFECTIVELY')

*[Further reading recommendations are indicated with an asterisk.]*

Bennett, J., Lubben, F., & Hogarth, S. (2006) Bringing science to life: A synthesis of the research evidence on the effects of context-based and STS approaches to science teaching. *Science Education*, 91(1), 36–74. Accessible from: https://www.york.ac.uk/media/educationalstudies/documents/staff-docs/Bennett%20Lubben%20Hogarth%202007.pdf

*Carroll, J., Bradley, L., Crawford, H., Hannant, P., Johnson, H., & Thompson, A. (2017). SEN Support: A Rapid Evidence Assessment. Accessible from: https://assets.publishing.service.gov.uk/government/uploads/system/uploads/attachment_data/file/628630/DfE_SEN_Support_REA_Report.pdf

Chapman, R. L., Buckley, L., & Sheehan, M. (2013) School-Based programs for increasing connectedness and reducing risk behavior. *A Systematic Review*, 25(1), 95–114.

*Coe, R., Aloisi, C., Higgins, S., & Major, L. E. (2014) *What Makes Great Teaching. Review of the Underpinning Research*. Durham University. Accessible from: http://bit.ly/2OvmvKO

DuPaul, G. J., Belk, G. D., & Puzino, K. (2016) Evidence-Based interventions for attention deficit hyperactivity disorder in children and adolescents. *Handbook of Evidence-Based Interventions for Children and Adolescents*, 167.

Education Endowment Foundation (2018) Improving Secondary Science Guidance Report. Accessible from: https://educationendowmentfoundation.org.uk/tools/guidance-reports/ [retrieved 10 October 2018].

Education Endowment Foundation (2018) Sutton Trust-Education Endowment Foundation Teaching and Learning Toolkit. Accessible from: https://educationendowmentfoundation.org.uk/evidence-summaries/teaching-learning-toolkit/ [retrieved 10 October 2018].

Gutman, L., & Schoon, L. (2013) The Impact of Non-cognitive Skills on the Outcomes of Young People. Accessible from: https://educationendowmentfoundation.org.uk/public/files/Publications/EEF_Lit_Review_Non-CognitiveSkills.pdf [retrieved 10 October 2018].

*Institute of Education Sciences (2008) Reducing Behavior Problems in the Elementary School Classroom. Accessible from: https://ies.ed.gov/ncee/wwc/PracticeGuide/4

Kern, L., & Clemens, N. H. (2007) Antecedent strategies to promote appropriate classroom behavior. *Psychology in the Schools*, 44(1), 65–75. https://doi.org/10.1002/pits.20206

Lazowski, R. A., & Hulleman, C. S. (2016) Motivation interventions in education: A meta-analytic review. *Review of Educational Research*, 86(2), 602–640. https://doi.org/10.3102/0034654315617832

Mitchell, D. (2014). *What Really Works in Special and Inclusive Education*. Oxford: Routledge.

Sibieta, L., Greaves, E., & Sianesi, B. (2014) Increasing Pupil Motivation: Evaluation Report. Accessible from: https://educationendowmentfoundation.org.uk/projects-and-evaluation/projects/increasing-pupil-motivation/ [retrieved 10 October 2018].

Ursache, A., Blair, C., & Raver, C. C. (2012) The promotion of self-regulation as a means of enhancing school readiness and early achievement in children at risk for school failure. *Child Development Perspectives*, 6(2), 122–128.

Willingham, D. T. (2009) *Why Don't Students like School?* San Francisco, CA: Jossey-Bass.

Wubbels, T., Brekelmans, M., den Brok, P., Wijsman, L., Mainhard, T., & van Tartwijk, J. (2014) Teacher-student relationships and classroom management. In E. T. Emmer, E. Sabornie, C. Evertson, & C. Weinstein (Eds.). *Handbook of Classroom Management: Research, Practice, and Contemporary Issues* (2nd ed., pp. 363–386). New York, NY: Routledge.

Yeager, D. S., & Walton, G. M. (2011) Social-psychological interventions in education: They're not magic. *Review of Educational Research*, 81(2), 267–301. https://doi.org/10.3102/0034654311405999

# PROFESSIONAL BEHAVIOURS (STANDARD 8 – 'FULFIL WIDER PROFESSIONAL RESPONSIBILITIES')

*[Further reading recommendations are indicated with an asterisk.]*


Allen, J. P., Pianta, R. C., Gregory, A., Mikami, A. Y., & Lun, J. (2011) An interaction-based approach to enhancing secondary school instruction and student achievement. *Science*, 333(6045), 1034–1037. https://doi.org/10.1126/science.1207998

Basma, B., & Savage, R. (2018) Teacher professional development and student literacy growth: A systematic review and meta-analysis. *Education Psychology Review*, 30, 457. https://doi.org/10.1007/s10648-017-9416-4

Blatchford, P., Bassett, P., Brown, P., Martin, C., Russell, A., & Webster, R. (2009) Deployment and Impact of Support Staff in Schools: Characteristics, Working Conditions and Job Satisfaction of Support Staff in Schools. Accessible from: http://eprints.uwe.ac.uk/12342/

*Carroll, J., Bradley, L., Crawford, H., Hannant, P., Johnson, H., & Thompson, A. (2017) *SEN Support: A Rapid Evidence Assessment*. Accessible from: https://assets.publishing.service.gov.uk/government/uploads/system/uploads/attachment_data/file/628630/DfE_SEN_Support_REA_Report.pdf

*Cordingley, P., Higgins, S., Greany, T., Buckler, N., Coles-Jordan, D., Crisp, B., Saunders, L., & Coe, R. (2015) Developing Great Teaching. Accessible from: https://tdtrust.org/about/dgt. [retrieved 18 October 2018].

Department for Education (2018) Schools: Guide to the 0 to 25 SEND Code of Practice. Accessible from: https://assets.publishing.service.gov.uk/government/uploads/system/uploads/attachment_data/file/349053/Schools_Guide_to_the_0_to_25_SEND_Code_of_Practice.pdf [retrieved 18 October 2018].

*Education Endowment Foundation (2015) Making Best Use of Teaching Assistants Guidance Report. Accessible from: https://educationendowmentfoundation.org.uk/tools/guidance-reports/ [retrieved 10 October 2018].

Education Endowment Foundation (2018) Sutton Trust-Education Endowment Foundation Teaching and Learning Toolkit. Accessible from: https://educationendowmentfoundation.org.uk/evidence-summaries/teaching-learning-toolkit/ [retrieved 10 October 2018].

Hughes, D., Mann, A., Barnes, S., Baladuf, B., & McKeown, R. (2016). Careers education: International literature review. Accessible from: https://educationendowmentfoundation.org.uk/evidence-summaries/evidence-reviews/careers-education/ [retrieved 18 October 2018].

Kraft, M., Blazar, D., & Hogan, D. (2018) The effect of teacher coaching on instruction and achievement: A meta-analysis of the causal evidence. *Review of Educational Research*. https://doi.org/10.3102/0034654318759268

Skaalvik, E. M., & Skaalvik, S. (2017) Still motivated to teach? A study of school context variables, stress and job satisfaction among teachers in senior high school. *Social Psychology of Education*, 20(1), 15–37. https://doi.org/10.1007/s11218-016-9363-9

Wei, R. C., Darling-Hammond, L., Andree, A., Richardson, N., & Orphanos, S. (2009). *Professional Learning in the Learning Profession: A Status Report on Teacher Development in the United States and Abroad*. Dallas, TX: National Staff Development Council.

# INDEX